ACCESS TO SHAKESPEARE

The Tragedy of
Julius
Caesar

A Facing-pages Translation into Contemporary English

ACCESS TO SHAKESPEARE

The Tragedy of
Julius
Caesar

A Facing-pages Translation into Contemporary English

Edited by
Jonnie Patricia Mobley, Ph.D.
Drama Department
Cuesta College
San Luis Obispo, California

Lorenz Educational Publishers
P.O. Box 711030, Los Angeles, CA 90071-9625

Cover border taken from the First Folio (1623)

Cover design by Tamada Brown Design, Chicago

Interior design and typesetting by David Corona Design, Dubuque

Published by Lorenz Educational Publishers. © 1995 by Lorenz Educational Publishers, PO Box 711030, Los Angeles, California 90071-9625. All rights reserved. No part of this book may be reproduced, stored in a retrieval system, or transmitted in any form or by any means without the prior permission of Lorenz Educational Publishers.

ISBN: 1-885564-04-X

Library of Congress Card Catalog Card Number: 94-78621
Manufactured in the United States of America.
5 6 7 8 9 0 6 5 4 3 2 1

The Tragedy of
Julius
Caesar

Contents

Introduction

This volume of William Shakespeare's *The Tragedy of Julius Caesar* consists of two versions of the play. The first is the original, based on the *Globe* edition of 1860, which was in turn based on the Folio of 1623. The second version is a translation of the original into contemporary English. In both versions spelling and punctuation have been updated, and the names of the characters have been spelled out in full for easier reading. Insights from modern scholars have been included in both versions.

The translation of *Julius Caesar* is not meant to take the place of the original. Instead, it is an alternative to the notes usually included in modern editions. In many editions these notes interfere with the reading of the play. Whether alongside or below the original text, the notes break the rhythm of reading and frequently force the reader to turn back to an earlier page or jump ahead to a later one. Having a translation that runs parallel to the original, line for line, allows the reader to move easily from Elizabethan to contemporary English and back again. It's simply a better way to introduce Shakespeare.

Also, this translation is suitable for performance, where notes are not available to the audience. Admittedly, a well-directed and well-acted production can do much to clarify Shakespeare's language. And yet, there will be numerous references and lines whose meanings are not accessible on a first hearing to many. What, for instance, does Caesar mean when he asks Casca, "Doth not Brutus bootless kneel?"

Shakespeare's Language

Shakespeare's language does present problems for modern readers. After all, four centuries separate us from him. During this time words have acquired new meanings or have dropped from the language altogether, and sentence structures have become less fluid. But these are solvable problems.

First of all, most of the words that Shakespeare used are still current. For those words whose meanings have changed and for those words no longer in the language, modern equivalents are found in this translation. For a small number of words—chiefly names of places, classical and mythological characters, and formal titles—a glossary can be found on page 207.

The meaning of words is one problem. The position of words is another. Today, the order of words in declarative sentences is almost fixed. The subject comes first, then the verb, and finally, if there is one, the object. In Shakespeare's time, the order of words, particularly in poetic drama, was more fluid. Shakespeare has Brutus say:

> How I have thought of this, and of these times,
> I shall recount hereafter.

Whereas we would usually arrange the words in the following order:

> I shall recount hereafter
> How I have thought of this, and of these times.

Later in the play, Brutus says:

> Such an exploit have I in hand...

We would probably say:

> I have such an exploit in hand...

This does not mean that Shakespeare never uses words in what we would consider normal order. As often as not, he does. Here, for instance, are Caesar and Brutus in conversation:

> BRUTUS   A soothsayer bids you beware the ides of March.
> CAESAR   Set him before me. Let me see his face.

When Shakespeare does invert the order of words, he does so for a reason or for a variety of reasons—to create a rhythm, to emphasize a word, to achieve a rhyme. Whether a play is in verse, as most of this play is, or in prose, it is still written in sentences. And that means, despite the order, all the words needed to make complete sentences are there. If you are puzzled by a sentence, first look for the subject and then try rearranging the words in the order that you would normally use. It takes a little practice, but you will be surprised how quickly you acquire the skill.

Shakespeare sometimes separates sentence parts—parts of a verb, for example—that would normally be run together. Here are some lines that Cassius speaks to Brutus:

> ...as Aeneas, our great ancestor,
> Did from the flames of Troy upon his shoulder
> The old Anchises bear...

Between the auxiliary *did* and the main verb *bear* come three prepositional phrases and a direct object that interrupt the normal sequence. Again, look for the separated parts and put them together. Here, for example, is Brutus speaking of his ancestors:

> My ancestors did from the streets of Rome
> The Tarquin drive when he was called a king.

Joining the two parts of the verb, you might arrive at the following:

> My ancestors did drive the Tarquin
> From the streets of Rome when he was called a king.

You'll find, however, that your rearranged sentence, while clear, is not as rhythmical as Shakespeare's.

Stage Directions

In drama written for the modern stage, the playwright usually provides detailed directions for the actors—how to move and speak, what emotions to convey to an audience. In Shakespeare's plays, stage directions are sparse. One reason could be that Shakespeare was a member and an owner of the company for which he wrote these plays. He was on hand to tell the other actors how to say a line or what gesture to use. Even so, the dialogue itself offers clues to actions or gestures. For example, Brutus, in Act Four, is in a heated argument with Cassius about bribes in their army. He says:

> ...shall we now
> Contaminate our fingers with base bribes
> And sell the mighty space of our large honors
> For so much trash as may be grasped thus?

At this point, Brutus probably makes a fist—a contrast to "the mighty space of our large honors." Again, in Act Three, Mark Antony says:

> You all do know this mantle.

And he probably picks up Caesar's bloody cloak. He goes on,

> Look, in this place ran Cassius' dagger through.
> See what a rent the envious Casca made.

These lines call for gestures by the actor playing Antony, but, lacking written stage directions, one can't be sure exactly what these gestures are.

Reading the printed play, you must keep in mind that the dialogue was written to be spoken by actors who move about a stage—gesturing, drawing swords, reading letters, weeping, and laughing. In a sense, you must learn to stage the play in your imagination. You must picture in your head, for example, the circle of assassins gathered about Caesar, fawning but ready to strike. For many, this imaginative reading of Shakespeare is the most satisfying.

Solo Speeches

There is another difference between the plays of Shakespeare and most modern ones—the solo speeches. These are the asides and the soliloquies in which a character reveals what is on his or her mind. Modern dramatists seem to feel that the solo speech is artificial and unrealistic. Oddly enough, modern novelists frequently use a variety of the solo speech, and some critics feel that this convention has given the novel extra power and depth, allowing it to probe deeply into the motives of its characters. One thing is certain—Shakespeare's plays without the solo speeches would lack the power we have come to know.

The Tragedy of
Julius
Caesar

Characters

JULIUS CAESAR
CALPURNIA, wife of Caesar

MARK ANTONY
OCTAVIUS CAESAR } ruling triumvirs after Julius
LEPIDUS   } Caesar's death

MARCUS BRUTUS
CAIUS CASSIUS
CASCA
DECIUS BRUTUS   } conspirators against
CINNA   } Julius Caesar
TREBONIUS
METELLUS CIMBER
CAIUS LIGARIUS

FLAVIUS   } tribunes critical of
MARULLUS   } Julius Caesar

ARTEMIDORUS   } a teacher and a soothsayer
FORTUNE-TELLER   } who try to warn Julius Caesar

CICERO
PUBLIUS CIMBER   } senators
POPILIUS LENA

CINNA, a poet
PORTIA, wife of Brutus
LUCIUS, boy attendant of Brutus
PINDARUS, servant of Cassius

LUCILIUS, TITINIUS, MESSALA, YOUNG CATO,
    VOLUMNIUS, friends of Brutus and Cassius

VARRO, CLITUS, CLAUDIUS, STRATO, DARDANIUS,
    servants or officers of Brutus

SENATORS, CITIZENS, GUARDS, ATTENDANTS,
    SOLDIERS, POET, SERVANT, and GHOST

Act One

Scene 1 [*A street in Rome.*] *Enter* FLAVIUS, MARULLUS, *and* CERTAIN
  CITIZENS

FLAVIUS Hence! Home, you idle creatures, get you home.
  Is this a holiday? What, know you not,
  Being mechanical, you ought not walk
  Upon a laboring day without the sign
  Of your profession? Speak, what trade art thou?   5

FIRST CITIZEN Why, sir, a carpenter.

MARULLUS Where is thy leather apron and thy rule?
  What dost thou with thy best apparel on?
  You, sir, what trade are you?

SECOND CITIZEN Truly, sir, in respect of a fine workman, I am but,   10
  as you would say, a cobbler.

MARULLUS But what trade are thou? Answer me directly.

SECOND CITIZEN A trade, sir, that I hope I may use with a safe
  conscience; which is indeed, sir, a mender of bad soles.

MARULLUS What trade, thou knave? Thou naughty nave,   15
  what trade?

SECOND CITIZEN Nay, sir, I beseech you, be not out with me; yet
  if you be out, sir, I can mend you.

MARULLUS What meanest thou by that? Mend me, thou saucy fellow?

SECOND CITIZEN Why, sir, cobble you.   20

FLAVIUS Thou are a cobbler, art thou?

SECOND CITIZEN Truly, sir, all that I live by is with the awl. I meddle
  with no tradesman's matters, nor women's matters; but withal I am
  indeed, sir, a surgeon to old shoes; when they are in great danger, I
  recover them. As proper men as ever trod upon neat's leather have   25

2

Act One

Scene 1 [*A street in Rome.*] *Enter* FLAVIUS, MARULLUS, and CERTAIN
CITIZENS

FLAVIUS Now, go home, you idle creatures, go home.
    What is this, a holiday? Don't you know
    That workers should wear working clothes
    In the street on a weekday? You there,
    Tell me, what is your trade?   5

FIRST CITIZEN Me, sir? Why I'm a carpenter.

MARULLUS Then where is your leather apron and your ruler?
    What are you doing with your best clothes on?
    You, sir, what is your trade?

SECOND CITIZEN Actually, sir, compared to a real tradesman, I just,   10
    as you would say, fix things.

MARULLUS But what is your trade? Answer me plainly.

SECOND CITIZEN A trade, sir, that I can practice with a clear
    conscience. I am, indeed, sir, a mender of bad soles.

MARULLUS What trade, you worthless clod? Fool, what is   15
    your trade?

SECOND CITIZEN Please, I ask you, sir, don't be out of sorts. But
    if you are, sir, I can fix that too.

MARULLUS What do you mean by that? Fix what, you uppity fellow?

SECOND CITIZEN Why, sir, I can cobble you.   20

FLAVIUS You are a cobbler, are you?

SECOND CITIZEN Truly, sir, all my living is based on the awl. I
    don't meddle in tradesmen's affairs, nor in affairs with women,
    but, after all, I am a surgeon of shoes. When their lives are in danger,
    I save them. As good a man who ever walked on shoe leather   25

gone upon my handiwork.

FLAVIUS But wherefore art thou not in thy shop today?

Why dost thou lead these men about the streets?

SECOND CITIZEN Truly, sir, to wear out their shoes, to get

myself into more work. But indeed, sir, we make holiday   30

to see Caesar, and to rejoice in his triumph.

MARULLUS Wherefore rejoice? What conquest brings he home?

What tributaries follow him to Rome,

To grace in captive bonds his chariot-wheels?   35

You blocks, you stones, you worse than senseless things!

O you hard hearts, you cruel men of Rome,

Knew you not Pompey? Many a time and oft

Have you climbed up to walls and battlements,

To towers and windows, yea, to chimney-tops,   40

Your infants in your arms, and there have sat

The livelong day, with patient expectation,

To see great Pompey pass the streets of Rome.

And when you saw his chariot but appear,

Have you not made an universal shout,   45

That Tiber trembled underneath her banks

To hear the replication of your sounds

Made in her concave shores?

And do you now put on your best attire?

And do you now cull out a holiday?   50

And do you now strew flowers in his way

That comes in triumph over Pompey's blood?

Be gone!

Run to your houses, fall upon your knees,

4

has trod on my handiwork.

FLAVIUS But why aren't you in your shop today?

Why do you lead these men around the streets?

SECOND CITIZEN Actually, sir, to wear out their shoes, so I'll have

more work. But seriously, sir, we've taken the day off to see   30

Caesar and celebrate his victory.

MARULLUS What is there to celebrate? What treasure does he bring home?

What hostages has he brought to Rome,

Chained in honor to his chariot wheels?   35

You blocks, you stones, you worse than senseless things!

Oh, you hard-hearted, cruel men of Rome,

Have you forgotten Pompey? Many times and often

Have you climbed up walls and battlements,

To towers and windows, even to the tops of chimneys,   40

Your infants in your arms, and there have sat

The whole long day, in patient expectation,

To see great Pompey pass the streets of Rome.

And when you saw his chariot first appear,

Did you not send up a universal cheer,   45

Making the River Tiber tremble beneath its banks

To hear the echoes of your shouts

Made along its curving shores?

And are you now wearing your best clothes?

And are you now giving yourself a holiday?   50

And are you now throwing flowers in the path

Of him that comes in triumph over Pompey's sons?

Be gone!

Run home and fall on your knees.

Pray to the gods to intermit the plague   55
That needs must light on this ingratitude.
FLAVIUS Go, go, good countrymen, and for this fault
Assemble all the poor men of your sort;
Draw them to the Tiber banks, and weep your tears
Into the channel, till the lowest stream   60
Do kiss the most exalted shore of all.

                                Exeunt all CITIZENS

See whe'r their basest mettle be not moved.
They vanish tongue-tied in their guiltiness.
Go you down that way towards the Capitol;
This way will I. Disrobe the images,   65
If you do find them decked with ceremonies.
MARULLUS May we do so?
You know it is the Feast of Lupercal.
FLAVIUS It is no matter. Let no images
Be hung with Caesar's trophies. I'll about   70
And drive away the vulgar from the streets.
So do you too, where you perceive them thick.
These growing feathers plucked from Caesar's wing
Will make him fly an ordinary pitch,
Who else would soar above the ordinary view of men,   75
And keep us all in servile fearfulness.

                                Exeunt

Scene 2 [*A crowded square in Rome*]
Trumpet fanfare offstage. Enter CAESAR, *his wife* CALPURNIA, ANTONY,
BRUTUS, *his wife* PORTIA, DECIUS, CICERO, CASSIUS, CASCA, SOOTHSAYER,
MARULLUS, *and* FLAVIUS

Pray that the gods suspend the plague   55

That should punish such ingratitude.

FLAVIUS   Go, go, good countrymen. To remedy this fault,

Assemble all the poor men of your class,

Lead them to the banks of the Tiber, and cry

Until your tears flood the lowest streams   60

So that they kiss the highest shore.

Exit all CITIZENS

See, even their leaden natures are moved.

They vanish tongue-tied, covered with guilt.

You go down that way, towards the Capitol;

I'll go this way. If you find statues of Caesar   65

With decorations, remove them.

MARULLUS   Do you think we dare?

You know, it is the Feast of Lupercal.

FLAVIUS   It doesn't matter. Let no statues

Be hung with Caesar's decorations. I'll go around   70

And order the common people off the streets.

You do the same, where you see them gathered.

These growing feathers plucked from Caesar's wing

Will make him fly at a normal height;

Otherwise, he would soar beyond human sight   75

And keep us all in slavish dread.

Exit

Scene 2   [*A crowded square in Rome*]

Trumpet fanfare offstage. Enter CAESAR, *his wife* CALPURNIA, ANTONY, BRUTUS, *his wife* PORTIA, DECIUS, CICERO, CASSIUS, CASCA, *a* FORTUNE-TELLER, MARULLUS, *and* FLAVIUS

CAESAR Calpurnia!

CASCA Peace, ho! Caesar speaks.

CAESAR Calpurnia.

CALPURNIA Here, my lord.

CAESAR Stand you directly in Antonius' way   5

    When he doth run his course. Antonius!

ANTONY Caesar, my lord?

CAESAR Forget not in your speed, Antonius,

    To touch Calpurnia; for our elders say,

    The barren, touched in this holy chase   10

    Shake off their sterile curse.

ANTONY I shall remember.

    When Caesar says "Do this," it is performed.

CAESAR Set on, and leave no ceremony out.

Music.

SOOTHSAYER Caesar!   15

CAESAR Ha! Who calls?

CASCA Bid every noise be still. Peace yet again!

CAESAR Who is it in the press that calls on me?

    I hear a tongue, shriller than all the music,

    Cry "Caesar!" Speak, Caesar is turned to hear.   20

SOOTHSAYER Beware the ides of March.

CAESAR What man is that?

BRUTUS A soothsayer bids you beware the ides of March.

CAESAR Set him before me. Let me see his face.

CASSIUS Fellow, come from the throng. Look upon Caesar.   25

CAESAR What sayst thou to me now? Speak once again.

SOOTHSAYER Beware the ides of March.

CAESAR Calpurnia!

CASCA Silence! Caesar speaks.

CAESAR Calpurnia.

CALPURNIA Here, my lord.

CAESAR Stand directly in Antony's way   5
    When he runs in the Lupercal race. Antony!

ANTONY Caesar, my lord?

CAESAR Don't forget in your haste, Antony,
    To touch Calpurnia. Our wise men say
    Barren women, touched in this holy race,   10
    Are cured of their sterility.

ANTONY I shall remember.
    When Caesar says, "Do this!" it is done.

CAESAR Proceed, and leave no ceremony out.

Music.

FORTUNE-TELLER Caesar!   15

CAESAR What? Who calls?

CASCA Stop this noise! Silence again!

CAESAR Who is it in that throng that calls me?
    I hear a voice cutting through all the music
    Cry "Caesar!" Speak! Caesar has turned to hear.   20

FORTUNE-TELLER Beware the ides of March.

CAESAR Who is that man?

BRUTUS A fortune-teller who advises you beware the ides of March.

CAESAR Bring him here before me. Let me see his face.

CASSIUS Fellow, come up from the crowd. Behold Caesar.   25

CAESAR Now what do you have to say to me? Speak once again.

FORTUNE-TELLER Beware the ides of March.

CAESAR He is a dreamer. Let us leave him. Pass.
Sennet.

Exeunt all but BRUTUS *and* CASSIUS

CASSIUS Will you go see the order of the course?
BRUTUS Not I.   30
CASSIUS I pray you do.
BRUTUS I am not gamesome. I do lack some part
    Of that quick spirit that is in Antony.
    Let me not hinder, Cassius, your desires.
    I'll leave you.   35
CASSIUS Brutus, I do observe you now of late;
    I have not from your eyes that gentleness
    And show of love as I was wont to have.
    You bear too stubborn and too strange a hand
    Over your friend that loves you.   40
BRUTUS Cassius,
    Be not deceived. If I have veiled my look,
    I turn the trouble of my countenance
    Merely upon myself. Vexed I am
    Of late with passions of some difference,   45
    Conceptions only proper to myself,
    Which give some soil, perhaps, to my behaviors.
    But let not therefore my good friends be grieved—
    Among which number, Cassius, be you one—
    Nor construe any further my neglect   50
    Than that poor Brutus, with himself at war,
    Forgets the shows of love to other men.
CASSIUS Then, Brutus, I have much mistook your passion,

CAESAR He is a dreamer. Let us leave him. Proceed.

Trumpet flourish.

Exit all but BRUTUS *and* CASSIUS

CASSIUS Will you go to watch the race?

BRUTUS Not I.   30

CASSIUS Please do.

BRUTUS I am not much for games. I am afraid I lack

  That lively spirit that is in Antony.

  But, Cassius, don't let me stop you from going.

  I'll leave you now.   35

CASSIUS Brutus, I have been observing you lately;

  I have not seen that warmth in your eyes

  That I had become accustomed to.

  Your manner has been cool and distant

  Toward your old friend, who loves you.   40

BRUTUS Cassius,

  Don't be misled. If my looks are clouded,

  My frowns have been directed only at what

  I see in myself. I am troubled

  Lately by conflicting emotions,   45

  Thoughts that concern only me,

  Which give a blemish, perhaps, to my behavior.

  I don't want to upset my good friends—

  Among whom, Cassius, I count you—

  Nor believe that my aloofness has any other reason   50

  Than the conflict that is going on inside me,

  Which makes me unsociable.

CASSIUS Then, Brutus, I have misread your feelings,

By means whereof this breast of mine hath buried

Thoughts of great value, worthy cogitations.   55

Tell me, good Brutus, can you see your face?

BRUTUS No, Cassius; for the eye sees not itself

But by reflection, by some other things.

CASSIUS 'Tis just;

And it is very much lamented, Brutus,   60

That you have no such mirrors as will turn

Your hidden worthiness into your eye,

That you might see your shadow. I have heard

Where many of the best respect in Rome—

Except immortal Caesar—speaking of Brutus,   65

And groaning underneath this age's yoke,

Have wished that noble Brutus had his eyes.

BRUTUS Into what dangers would you lead me, Cassius,

That you would have me seek into myself

For that which is not in me?   70

CASSIUS Therefore, good Brutus, be prepared to hear.

And since you know you cannot see yourself

So well as by reflection, I, your glass

Will modestly discover to yourself

That of yourself which yet you know not of.   75

And be not jealous on me, gentle Brutus.

Were I a common laughter, or did use

To stale with ordinary oaths my love

To every new protester; if you know

That I do fawn on men, and hug them hard,   80

And after scandal them; or if you know

And as a result have kept to myself
My own deep and innermost thoughts.   55
Tell me, good Brutus, can you see your face?

BRUTUS   No, Cassius, for the eye can see itself
Only by reflection, by using other things.

CASSIUS   That's right!
And it is greatly regretted, Brutus,   60
That you have no such mirror as will show
Your inner qualities to your own eyes,
That you might see them in a reflection. I have heard
Many Romans of the highest reputation—
Except the immortal Caesar—speak of Brutus,   65
When complaining of the oppression of this time,
And wish that the noble Brutus were not so blind.

BRUTUS   Into what dangers are you leading me, Cassius,
That you would have me look into myself
For things that are not there?   70

CASSIUS   And so, good Brutus, listen while I explain.
And since you know you cannot see yourself
Except by reflection, I'll be your mirror
And faithfully reveal to you things
About yourself that even you do not know.   75
And don't be suspicious of me, noble Brutus.
Were I a scatterbrain, or if I
Cheapened my friendship by offering it
To every new acquaintance, if you know
That I flattered men, hugged them hard,   80
And later slandered them, or if you know

13

That I profess myself in banqueting

To all the rout, then hold me dangerous.

Flourish, and shout.

BRUTUS What means this shouting? I do fear the people

Choose Caesar for their king.   85

CASSIUS Ay, do you fear it?

Then must I think you would not have it so.

BRUTUS I would not, Cassius, yet I love him well.

But wherefore do you hold me here so long?

What is it that you would impart to me?   90

If it be aught toward the general good,

Set honor in one eye, and death i' th' other,

And I will look on both indifferently;

For let the gods so speed me as I love

The name of honor more than I fear death.   95

CASSIUS I know that virtue to be in you, Brutus,

As well as I do know your outward favor.

Well, honor is the subject of my story.

I cannot tell what you and other men

Think of this life; but for my single self,   100

I had as lief not be as live to be

In awe of such a thing as I myself.

I was born free as Caesar, so were you;

We have both fed as well, and we can both

Endure the winter's cold as well as he.   105

For once, upon a raw and gusty day,

The troubled Tiber chafing with her shores,

Caesar said to me "Dar'st thou, Cassius, now

That I proclaim my friendship with all the rabble

When I'm out drinking, then consider me dangerous.

Trumpets sound, and shouts are heard.

BRUTUS What's the meaning of those shouts? I fear the people

Have chosen Caesar as their king. 85

CASSIUS Yes, do you fear it?

Then I must believe you would not wish it to happen.

BRUTUS I would not, Cassius, though I revere him.

But why do you hold me here so long?

What is it that you're trying to tell me? 90

If it has anything to do with the good of the people,

Put honor in one eye and death in the other,

And I will look upon both impartially;

For the gods help me prosper, in that I love

The name of honor more than I fear death. 95

CASSIUS I know that quality is within you, Brutus,

As well as I recognize your appearance.

Well, honor is the subject of my story.

I am not sure what you and other men

May think of life; but as for me, 100

I would as soon be dead as live

In awe of another man no different from myself.

I was born as free as Caesar, so were you;

We have both been fed as well, and we both can

Endure the cold of winter as well as he. 105

Once, upon a cold and windy day,

When the rough Tiber raged against its shores,

Caesar said to me, "Do you dare, Cassius,

Leap in with me into this angry flood
And swim to yonder point?" Upon the word,   110
Accoutred as I was, I plunged in
And bade him follow; so indeed he did.
The torrent roared, and we did buffet it
With lusty sinews, throwing it aside,
And stemming it with hearts of controversy.   115
But ere we could arrive the point proposed,
Caesar cried "Help me, Cassius, or I sink!"
I, as Aeneas, our great ancestor,
Did from the flames of Troy upon his shoulder
The old Anchises bear, so from the waves of Tiber   120
Did I the tired Caesar. And this man
Is now become a god, and Cassius is
A wretched creature, and must bend his body
If Caesar carelessly but nod on him.
He had a fever when he was in Spain,   125
And when the fit was on him I did mark
How he did shake. 'Tis true, this god did shake!
His coward lips did from their color fly,
And that same eye whose bend doth awe the world
Did lose his luster. I did hear him groan—   130
Ay, and that tongue of his that bade the Romans
Mark him, and write his speeches in their books,
Alas, it cried "Give me some drink, Titinius,"
As a sick girl. Ye gods, it doth amaze me
A man of such feeble temper should   135
So get the start of the majestic world

To leap into this stormy sea with me
And swim to that farther point?" Upon that word,   110
With my armor on, I plunged in
And told him to follow. So indeed he did.
The torrent roared, and we fought it
With vigorous strokes, pushing it aside,
Making headway against the waves, in our rivalry.   115
But before we could reach the point we'd chosen,
Caesar cried, "Help me, Cassius, or I'll drown."
Then I, like our great ancestor Aeneas,
Who bore his father Anchises from the flames of Troy
On his shoulders, saved from the waves of the Tiber   120
The tired Caesar. And this is the man
Who has now become a god, and Cassius is
A wretched puppet who must bow
If Caesar carelessly nods to him.
He had a fever when he was in Spain,   125
And when it was at its worst, I noticed
How he did shake. It's true, this god did shake!
The color fled from his cowardly lips,
And that same eye whose stare awes the world
Lost its sparkle. I heard him groan—   130
Yes, and that tongue of his that called on Romans
To take note of him and copy his speeches in their books,
Alas, it cried, "Give me some water, Titinius,"
Like a sick girl. Ye gods, it amazes me
That a man of such feeble temperament should   135
Leap ahead of the whole world of noble men

And bear the palm alone.

Flourish, shout.

BRUTUS Another general shout?

    I do believe that these applauses are

    For some new honors heaped on Caesar.   140

CASSIUS Why, man, he doth bestride the narrow world

    Like a colossus, and we petty men

    Walk under his huge legs and peep about

    To find ourselves dishonorable graves.

    Men at some time are masters of their fates.   145

    The fault, dear Brutus, is not in our stars,

    But in ourselves, that we are underlings.

    "Brutus" and "Caesar": what should be in that "Caesar"?

    Why should that name be sounded more than yours?

    Write them together, yours is as fair a name.   150

    Sound them, it doth become the mouth as well.

    Weigh them, it is as heavy. Conjure with 'em,

    "Brutus" will start a spirit as soon as "Caesar."

    Now in the names of all the gods at once,

    Upon what meat doth this our Caesar feed   155

    That he has grown so great? Age, thou are shamed!

    Rome, thou hast lost the breed of noble bloods!

    When went there by an age, since the great flood,

    But it was famed with more than one man?

    When could they say, till now, that talked of Rome,   160

    That her wide walks encompassed but one man?

    Now it is Rome indeed, and room enough,

    When there is in it but only one man.

And carry off the prize for himself.

The sound of trumpets, more shouts.

BRUTUS Another roar from the crowd?

    I begin to think the applause is

    For some new honors heaped on Caesar. 140

CASSIUS Why, man, he straddles the narrow world

    Like a colossus, and we lesser men

    Walk under his huge legs and peep around,

    Going to our graves dishonored.

    Men were at one time masters of their fates. 145

    The fault, dear Brutus, is not in our stars,

    But in ourselves, that we are inferiors.

    "Brutus" and "Caesar"—what special power's in that "Caesar"?

    Why should that name be uttered more than yours?

    Write them side by side, yours looks as fair. 150

    Speak them, and yours is as pleasant to say.

    Weigh them, yours is of equal weight. Conjure with them,

    "Brutus" will call up a spirit as soon as "Caesar."

    In the names of all the gods together,

    On what food does this our Caesar feed 155

    To make him grow so great? This shameful age in which we live!

    Rome, you no longer breed men of courageous spirit!

    When was there an age, since the great flood,

    That was not famous for more than one man?

    When could it be said, till now, that the wide walks 160

    Of Rome enclosed only one man?

    Rome is rightly named, and room enough,

    When there is in it only one man.

O, you and I have heard our fathers say,
There was a Brutus once that would have brooked 165
Th' eternal devil to keep his state in Rome
As easily as a king.

BRUTUS That you do love me, I am nothing jealous.
What you would work me to, I have some aim.
How I have thought of this, and of these times, 170
I shall recount hereafter. For this present,
I would not, so with love I might entreat you,
Be any further moved. What you have said
I will consider; what you have to say
I will with patience hear, and find a time 175
Both meet to hear and answer such high things.
Till then, my noble friend, chew on this:
Brutus had rather be a villager
Than to repute himself a son of Rome
Under these hard conditions as this time 180
Is like to lay upon us.

CASSIUS I am glad
That my weak words have struck but thus much show
Of fire from Brutus.

Enter CAESAR *and his train*

BRUTUS The games are done, and Caesar is returning. 185

CASSIUS As they pass by, pluck Casca by the sleeve,
And he will, after his sour fashion, tell you
What hath proceeded worthy note today.

BRUTUS I will do so. But look you, Cassius,
The angry spot doth glow on Caesar's brow, 190

Oh, you and I have heard our fathers say,
There was once a Brutus who would have let 165
The eternal devil rule in Rome
As readily as tolerate a king.

BRUTUS That you hold me in high regard, I do not doubt.
What you would have me do, I can partly guess.
What my thoughts are on this and on these times, 170
I shall tell you later on. For the present,
I would not, and I ask you as a friend,
Be urged any more. What you have said,
I will consider; what you have to say,
I will with patience hear, and find a time 175
That is appropriate to discuss such important matters.
Till then, my noble friend, think about this:
Brutus would rather live in some remote village
Than call himself a citizen of Rome
Under such oppression as the present conditions 180
Are likely to inflict on us.

CASSIUS I am glad
That my weak words have excited at least this much show
Of enthusiasm from you, Brutus.

Enter CAESAR *and his attendants*

BRUTUS The games have ended, and Caesar is returning. 185

CASSIUS As they pass, grab hold of Casca,
And he will, in his surly manner, tell you
What happened that is worth noting today.

BRUTUS I will do so. But look now, Cassius,
Caesar's brow glows with anger, 190

And all the rest look like a chidden train.
Calpurnia's cheek is pale, and Cicero
Looks with such ferret and such fiery eyes
As we have seen him in the Capitol,
Being crossed in conference by some senators.   195
CASSIUS Casca will tell us what the matter is.
CAESAR Antonius!
ANTONY Caesar?
CAESAR Let me have men about me that are fat,
Sleek-headed men, and such as sleep a-nights.   200
Yon Cassius has a lean and hungry look;
He thinks too much. Such men are dangerous.
ANTONY Fear him not, Caesar, he's not dangerous;
He is a noble Roman, and well given.
CAESAR Would he were fatter! But I fear him not.   205
Yet if my name were liable to fear,
I do not know the man I should avoid
So soon as that spare Cassius. He reads much,
He is a great observer, and he looks
Quite through the deeds of men. He loves no plays,   210
As thou dost, Antony; he hears no music.
Seldom he smiles, and smiles in such a sort
As if he mocked himself, and scorned his spirit
That could be moved to smile at anything.
Such men as he be never at heart's ease   215
Whiles they behold a greater than themselves,
And therefore are they very dangerous.
I rather tell thee what is to be feared

And all the rest look rebuked.

Calpurnia's cheek is pale, and Cicero,

With bloodshot and darting eyes like a ferret,

Looks as he does in the Capitol,

When some senators argue with him.   195

CASSIUS Casca will tell us what the matter is.

CAESAR Antony!

ANTONY Caesar?

CAESAR Let me be surrounded by fat men

With smooth-combed hair, the kind who sleep at night.   200

That Cassius has a lean and hungry look;

He thinks too much. Such men are dangerous.

ANTONY Fear him not, Caesar. He's not dangerous;

He is a noble Roman and very steady.

CAESAR I wish he were fatter, but I do not fear him.   205

Yet if Caesar were subject to fear,

I do not know the man I should avoid

So soon as that gaunt Cassius. He reads much,

He is a great observer, and he sees

Through the actions of men. He's no playgoer,   210

As you are, Antony; doesn't listen to music.

He seldom smiles, and when he does, it's in such a way

As if to mock himself, reproaching himself

That he could be moved to smile at anything.

Men like him are never content   215

So long as they see others above them.

And therefore they are very dangerous.

I tell you what is to be feared rather

Than what I fear; for always I am Caesar.

Come on my right hand, for this ear is deaf, 220

And tell me truly what thou think'st of him.

Sennet. Exit CAESAR *and his train, except* CASCA

CASCA You pulled me by the cloak. Would you speak with me?

BRUTUS Ay, Casca; tell us what hath chanced today

That Caesar looks so sad.

CASCA Why, you were with him, were you not? 225

BRUTUS I should not then ask Casca what had chanced.

CASCA Why, there was a crown offered him; and being offered

him, he put it by with the back of his hand, thus; and then

the people fell a-shouting.

BRUTUS What was the second noise for? 230

CASCA Why, for that too.

CASSIUS They shouted thrice. What was the last cry for?

CASCA Why, for that too.

BRUTUS Was the crown offered him thrice?

CASCA Ay, marry, was't, and he put it by thrice, every time 235

gentler than other; and at every putting-by, mine honest

neighbors shouted.

CASSIUS Who offered him the crown?

CASCA Why, Antony.

BRUTUS Tell us the manner of it, gentle Casca. 240

CASCA I can as well be hanged as tell the manner of it. It was

mere foolery; I did not mark it. I saw Mark Antony offer

him a crown; yet 'twas not a crown neither, 'twas one of

those coronets; and, as I told you, he put it by once; but

Than what I fear, for I am Caesar, always.

Come on my right side, for this ear is deaf,   220

And tell me truly what you think of him.

The sound of trumpets. Exit CAESAR *and his attendants, except* CASCA

CASCA You pulled my cloak. Did you want to speak with me?

BRUTUS Yes, Casca, tell us what happened today

To make Caesar look so grim.

CASCA Why, you were with him, were you not?   225

BRUTUS I should not ask you then, if I were.

CASCA Why, they offered him a crown, and when it was offered,

he brushed it aside with the back of his hand, like this, and

then the people all shouted.

BRUTUS What was the second noise for?   230

CASCA Why, for the same thing.

CASSIUS They shouted three times. What was the last cry for?

CASCA Again, for the same thing.

BRUTUS Was the crown offered him three times?

CASCA Yes, indeed, it was. And three times, he pushed it aside,   235

each time more gently than the last; at each refusal, my

honest fellow countrymen shouted.

CASSIUS Who offered him the crown?

CASCA Why, Antony.

BRUTUS Tell us how it was done, gentle Casca.   240

CASCA I'll be hanged if I can describe it properly. It was a lot

of foolishness. I didn't pay attention. I saw Mark Antony offer him

a crown. Actually, it wasn't a crown either, it was one of

those laurel wreaths, and, as I told you, he refused it once, but

for all that, to my thinking, he would fain have had it. Then   245
he offered it to him again; then he put it by again; but, to my
thinking, he was very loath to lay his fingers off it. And then
he offered it the third time; he put it the third time by; and still
as he refused it the rabblement hooted, and clapped their chopped
hands, and threw up their sweaty nightcaps, and uttered such   250
a deal of stinking breath because Caesar refused the crown that it
had almost choked Caesar, for he swounded and fell down at it.
And for my part, I durst not laugh, for fear of opening my lips
and receiving the bad air.

CASSIUS But soft, I pray you; what, did Caesar swound?   255

CASCA He fell down in the marketplace, and foamed at mouth, and
was speechless.

BRUTUS 'Tis very like; he hath the falling sickness.

CASSIUS No, Caesar hath it not; but you, and I,
And honest Casca, we have the falling sickness.   260

CASCA I know not what you mean by that, but I am sure Caesar fell
down. If the tag-rag people did not clap him and hiss him, according
as he pleased and displeased them, as they used to do in the theatre,
I am no true man.

BRUTUS What did he say when he came unto himself?   265

CASCA Mary, before he fell down, when he perceived the common herd
was glad he refused the crown, he plucked me ope his doublet and offered them his throat to cut. An I had been a man of any occupation,
if I would not have taken him at a word, I would I might go to hell
among the rogues. And so he fell. When he came to himself he   270
said, if he had done or said anything amiss, he desired their worships
to think it was his infirmity. Three or four wenches where I stood

for all of that, in my opinion, he really wanted to have it. Then   245
Antony offered it to him again. Again, he refused it, but, in my
opinion, he was very reluctant to let go of it. And then Antony
offered it a third time. He refused it a third time. And as he did
so, the mob hooted and clapped with their rough hands, and threw
their sweaty caps in the air, and exhaled so much stinking breath   250
because Caesar had refused the crown that it almost choked
Caesar, for he fainted and fell down at the smell. For myself,
I didn't dare laugh for fear of opening my mouth and breathing
the stench.

CASSIUS   Wait a minute, please. Did Caesar faint?   255

CASCA   He fell down in the marketplace and foamed at the mouth and
was speechless.

BRUTUS   It's likely that he suffers from falling-sickness.

CASSIUS   No, Caesar doesn't have it; you and I
And honest Casca who have fallen under his spell have it.   260

CASCA   I don't know what you mean by that, but I am sure Caesar fell
down. If the riffraff didn't cheer him or hiss him according to
whether they were pleased or displeased, as they do in the theatre,
I am not an honest man.

BRUTUS   What did he say when he came to?   265

CASCA   Indeed, before he fell down, when he perceived the common
herd was glad he refused the crown, he opened his collar and
offered them his throat to cut. Had I been a common man, I would
have taken him at his word and have gone to hell with all the
other rogues. And so, he fell. When he came to he said that   270
if he had done or said anything amiss, he hoped these gentlemen
would blame it on his disability. Three or four women where I stood

cried "Alas, good soul!" and forgave him with all their hearts. But there's no heed to be taken of them; if Caesar had stabbed their mothers they would have done no less.   275

BRUTUS And after that he came thus sad away?

CASCA Ay.

CASSIUS Did Cicero say anything?

CASCA Ay, he spoke Greek.

CASSIUS To what effect?   280

CASCA Nay, an I tell you that, I'll ne'er look you i' th' face again. But those that understood him smiled at one another and shook their heads; but for mine own part, it was Greek to me. I could tell you more news too: Marullus and Flavius, for pulling scarfs off Caesar's images, are put to silence. Fare you well. There was   285 more foolery yet, if I could remember it.

CASSIUS Will you sup with me tonight, Casca?

CASCA No, I am promised forth.

CASSIUS Will you dine with me tomorrow?

CASCA Ay, if I be alive, and your mind hold, and your dinner worth   290 the eating.

CASSIUS Good, I will expect you.

CASCA Do so. Farewell both.

Exit

BRUTUS What a blunt fellow is this grown to be!

He was quick mettle when he went to school.   295

CASSIUS So he is now in execution

Of any bold or noble enterprise,

However he puts on this tardy form.

This rudeness is a sauce to his good wit,

cried, "Oh, poor soul!" and forgave him with all their hearts.

But take no notice of them. If Caesar had stabbed their mothers,

they would have said the same thing.   275

BRUTUS   And after that, he came away looking grim.

CASCA   Yes.

CASSIUS   Did Cicero have anything to say?

CASCA   Yes, he spoke in Greek.

CASSIUS   To what effect?   280

CASCA   Now, if I could tell you that, I'd never look you in that face again.

But those who understood him smiled at one another and nodded

their heads. So far as I'm concerned, it was Greek to me. I can tell

you more news, too. Marullus and Flavius, for pulling decorations

off Caesar's statues, have been silenced. Farewell. There was more 285

foolishness still, if I could remember it.

CASSIUS   Will you have dinner with me tonight, Casca?

CASCA   No, I already have an engagement.

CASSIUS   Will you dine with me tomorrow?

CASCA   Yes, if I'm alive, and you haven't changed your mind, and   290

your dinner's worth eating.

CASSIUS   Good, I will expect you.

CASCA   Do so. Farewell to you both.

Exit CASCA

BRUTUS   What a blunt fellow he's grown to be.

He was a lively character even when he was in school.   295

CASSIUS   He still is when carrying out

Any bold or noble enterprise,

However much he adopts this slow-witted pretense.

His rough manner is a sauce to his shrewd remarks,

Which gives men stomach to digest his words   300
    With better appetite.
BRUTUS   And so it is. For this time I will leave you.
    Tomorrow, if you please to speak with me,
    I will come home to you: or, if you will,
    Come home to me, and I will wait for you.   305
CASSIUS   I will do so. Till then, think of the world.

> *Exit* BRUTUS

    Well, Brutus, thou are noble, yet I see
    Thy honorable mettle may be wrought
    From that it is disposed. Therefore it is meet
    That noble minds keep ever with their likes;   310
    For who so firm that cannot be seduced?
    Caesar doth bear me hard, but he loves Brutus.
    If I were Brutus now, and he were Cassius,
    He should not humor me. I will this night,
    In several hands, in at his windows throw,   315
    As if they came from several citizens,
    Writings, all tending to the great opinion
    That Rome holds of his name, wherein obscurely
    Caesar's ambition shall be glanced at.
    And after this let Caesar seat him sure,   320
    For we will shake him, or worse days endure.

> *Exit*

Scene 3 *Thunder and lightning. Enter* CASCA, *with a drawn sword, and*
    CICERO, *meeting*
CICERO   Good even, Casca. Brought you Caesar home?
    Why you are breathless, and why stare you so?

Which gives men the stomach to digest his words   300
    With better appetite.
BRUTUS And so it is. For now, I will leave you.
    Tomorrow, if you will talk more with me,
    I will come to your home. Or, if you wish,
    Come to my place, and I will be waiting for you.   305
CASSIUS I will do that. Till then, think about these things.

                   Exit BRUTUS

    Well, Brutus, you are noble. Yet I can see
    The essence of your honor may be twisted
    From its natural bent. For this reason, it is best
    That noble minds should mix only with their kind;   310
    For who's so firm that cannot be seduced?
    Caesar bears me ill will, but he likes Brutus.
    If I were Brutus now, and he were Cassius,
    Caesar should not influence me as he does. This night
    I will throw through Brutus' windows   315
    Letters in different handwriting, as though they came
    From different people, all referring to the high
    Reputation he has in Rome, with subtle hints
    Here and there of Caesar's ambition.
    And after that, Caesar had better make his seat secure,   320
    For we will shake him—or worse days we'll endure.

                   Exit

Scene 3 [*A street in Rome*] *Thunder and lightning. Enter* CASCA, *with a drawn sword, meeting* CICERO
CICERO Good evening, Casca. Have you taken Caesar home?
    Why are you out of breath and so wide-eyed?

CASCA Are you not moved, when all the sway of earth
　　　Shakes like a thing unfirm? O Cicero,
　　　I have seen tempests when the scolding winds　　　　　　5
　　　Have rived the knotty oaks, and I have seen
　　　Th' ambitious ocean swell, and rage, and foam,
　　　To be exalted with the threat'ning clouds;
　　　But never till tonight, never till now,
　　　Did I go through a tempest dropping fire.　　　　　　10
　　　Either there is a civil strife in heaven,
　　　Or else the world, too saucy with the gods,
　　　Incenses them to send destruction.
CICERO Why, saw you anything more wonderful?
CASCA A common slave—you know him well by sight—　　　15
　　　Held up his left hand, which did flame and burn
　　　Like twenty torches joined, and yet his hand,
　　　Not sensible of fire, remained unscorched.
　　　Besides—I ha'not since put up my sword—
　　　Against the capitol I met a lion,　　　　　　20
　　　Who glared upon me, and went surly by,
　　　Without annoying me. And there were drawn
　　　Upon a heap a hundred ghastly women,
　　　Transformed with their fear, who swore they saw
　　　Men, all in fire, walk up and down the streets.　　　25
　　　And yesterday the bird of night did sit,
　　　Even at noonday, upon the marketplace,
　　　Hooting and shrieking. When these prodigies
　　　Do so conjointly meet, let not men say
　　　"These are the reasons, they are natural";　　　　　　30

CASCA Aren't you upset when the whole world
    Shakes like some unstable thing? Oh, Cicero,
    I have seen storms whose raging winds   5
    Have split gnarled oaks, and I have seen
    The restless ocean swell and rage and foam,
    Raised high as the threatening heavens,
    But never till tonight, never till now,
    Did I experience a storm dropping fire.   10
    Either there is a civil war in heaven,
    Or else the world, too insolent for the gods,
    Incenses them to send destruction.
CICERO Well, what other wonders did you see?
CASCA A common slave—you know him well by sight—   15
    Held up his left hand, which burst into flame and burned
    Like twenty torches combined. And yet his hand
    Did not feel the flames and remained unburnt.
    Besides—I haven't sheathed my sword since—
    Near the Capitol I met a lion,   20
    Who stared at me and passed by in a lordly manner,
    But did me no harm. And there was a crowd
    Of a hundred women, looking like ghosts,
    Beside themselves with fear, who swore they saw
    Men, all on fire, walk up and down the streets.   25
    And yesterday, a bird of night sat
    At high noon in the marketplace,
    Hooting and shrieking. When all these strange events
    Come together at the same time, let men not say
    "There are causes, these are natural events";   30

For I believe they are portentous things

Unto the climate that they point upon.

CICERO Indeed it is a strange-disposed time.

But men may construe things after their fashion,

Clean from the purpose of the things themselves.   35

Comes Caesar to the Capitol tomorrow?

CASCA He doth, for he did bid Antonius

Send word to you he would be there tomorrow.

CICERO Good night then, Casca. This disturbed sky

Is not to walk in.   40

Exit CICERO

CASCA Farewell, Cicero

Enter CASSIUS

CASSIUS Who's there?

CASCA A Roman.

CASSIUS Casca, by your voice.

CASCA Your ear is good. Cassius, what night is this!   45

CASSIUS A very pleasing night to honest men.

CASCA Who ever knew the heavens menace so?

CASSIUS Those that have known the earth so full of faults.

For my part, I have walked about the streets,

Submitting me unto the perilous night   50

And thus unbraced, Casca, as you see,

Have bared my bosom to the thunderstone;

And when the cross blue lightning seemed to open

The breast of heaven, I did present myself

Even in the aim and very flash of it.   55

CASCA But wherefore did you so much tempt the heavens?

For I believe that they are ominous signs,

Directed at the region to which they point.

CICERO Indeed, it is a time of strange events.

But men interpret things in their own way,

Quite apart from their real meaning. 35

Will Caesar come to the Capitol tomorrow?

CASCA He will, for he has asked Antony

To send you word that he would be there.

CICERO Good night then, Casca. This stormy weather

Is not fit to walk in. 40

Exit CICERO

CASCA Farewell, Cicero.

Enter CASSIUS

CASSIUS Who's there?

CASCA A Roman.

CASSIUS It sounds like Casca.

CASCA Your hearing's good. What a night! 45

CASSIUS A very pleasant night for honest men.

CASCA Whoever saw the heavens so menacing?

CASSIUS Those who know that the earth is full of faults.

For my part, I have walked about the streets,

At the mercy of this dangerous night; 50

And with my shirt opened, Casca, as you see,

Have bared my chest to the thunderbolts;

And when the forked blue lightning seemed to open

The breast of heaven, I offered myself

Right in its path, its very flash. 55

CASCA But why did you provoke the heavens like this?

It is the part of men to fear and tremble
When the most mighty gods by tokens send
Such dreadful heralds to astonish us.

CASSIUS You are dull, Casca, and those sparks of life   60
    That should be in a Roman you do want
    Or else you use not. You look pale, and gaze,
    And put on fear, and cast yourself in wonder,
    To see the strange impatience of the heavens.
    But if you would consider the true cause   65
    Why all these fires, why all these gliding ghosts,
    Why birds and beasts, from quality and kind,
    Why old men, fools, and children calculate,
    Why all things change from their ordinance,
    Their natures and preformed faculties,   70
    To monstrous quality, why, you shall find
    That heaven hath infused them with these spirits
    To make them instruments of fear and warning
    Unto some monstrous state.
    Now could I, Casca, name to thee a man   75
    Most like this dreadful night,
    That thunders, lightens, opens graves, and roars
    As doth the lion in the Capitol;
    A man no mightier than thyself, or me,
    In personal action, yet prodigious grown,   80
    And fearful, as these strange eruptions are.
CASCA 'Tis Caesar that you mean. Is it not, Cassius?
CASSIUS Let it be who it is; for Romans now
    Have thews and limbs like to their ancestors;

It is the role of man to fear and tremble

When the most mighty gods send signs

Of what's to come to terrify us.

CASSIUS   You are slow, Casca. That spirit   60

That should be in every Roman you lack,

Or do not use. You look pale and stare

And show fear, work yourself into a state of amazement,

To see the strange restlessness of the heavens.

But if you would analyze the true cause—   65

Why there are all these fires, why all these gliding ghosts,

Why birds and beasts change their natures,

Why old men, fools, and children prophesy,

Why all things change their functions,

Their natures and their ordained qualities,   70

To unnatural behavior—why, you shall find

That heaven has infused them with these powers

As fearful warnings

Of an unnatural state of affairs.

Now I could, Casca, name you a man   75

Almost like this dreadful night

That thunders, lightens, opens graves, and roars

Like the lion in the Capitol;

A man no mightier than yourself, or me,

In his own deeds, yet one grown as ominous   80

And fearful as these unnatural outbreaks.

CASCA   It's Caesar that you mean; is it not, Cassius?

CASSIUS   Let it be who it is. Romans today

Have sinews and limbs just like their ancestors;

But, woe the while, our fathers' minds are dead, 85

And we are governed with our mothers' spirits.

Our yoke and sufferance show us womanish.

CASCA Indeed, they say the senators tomorrow

Mean to establish Caesar as a king,

And he shall wear his crown by sea and land 90

In every place save here in Italy.

CASSIUS I know where I will wear this dagger then;

Cassius from bondage will deliver Cassius.

Therein, ye gods, you make the weak most strong;

Therein, ye gods, you tyrants do defeat. 95

Nor stony tower, nor walls of beaten brass,

Nor airless dungeon, nor strong links of iron,

Can be retentive to the strength of spirit;

But life, being weary of these worldly bars,

Never lacks power to dismiss itself. 100

If I know this, know all the world besides,

That part of tyranny that I do bear

I can shake off at pleasure.

Thunder still.

CASCA So can I.

So every bondman in his own hand bears 105

The power to cancel his captivity.

CASSIUS And why should Caesar be a tyrant then?

Poor man, I know he would not be a wolf

But that he sees the Romans are but sheep.

He were no lion were not Romans hinds. 110

Those that with haste will make a mighty fire

But, alas for these times, our fathers' minds are dead,   85

And we are governed by our mothers' spirits.

Our burden and the way we suffer it make us mere women.

CASCA Indeed, they say the senators tomorrow

Mean to make Caesar a king,

And he shall wear his crown on land and sea,   90

Everywhere except here in Italy.

CASSIUS I know where I will sheath this dagger then;

Cassius from slavery will rescue Cassius.

By this means, you gods, you make weak men strong;

By this means, you gods, you defeat the tyrants.   95

No tower of stone nor wall of beaten brass,

No airless dungeon nor strong chains of iron

Can hold back a determined spirit;

For life, when weary of these worldly bonds,

Never lacks the power to free itself.   100

If I know this, let all the world know,

That any tyranny I suffer,

I can shake off at my pleasure.

The thunder continues.

CASCA So can I.

And so every prisoner has in his own hand   105

The power to escape his captivity.

CASSIUS So why should Caesar be a tyrant?

Poor man. I know he'd not be a wolf

Except that he sees the Romans are only sheep.

He would be no lion if the Romans were not deer.   110

Those who would make a mighty fire quickly

Begin it with weak straws. What trash is Rome,
What rubbish, and what offal, when it serves
For the base matter to illuminate
So vile a thing as Caesar! But, O grief,   115
Where hast thou led me? I perhaps speak this
Before a willing bondman; then I know
My answer must be made. But I am armed,
And dangers are to me indifferent.

CASCA You speak to Casca, and to such a man   120
    That is no fleering telltale. Hold, my hand.
    Be factious for redress of all these griefs,
    And I will set this foot of mine as far
    As who goes farthest.

CASSIUS There's a bargain made.   125
    Now know you, Casca, I have moved already
    Some certain of the noblest-minded Romans
    To undergo with me an enterprise
    Of honorable-dangerous consequence;
    And I do know, by this they stay for me   130
    In Pompey's porch; for now, this fearful night,
    There is no stir or walking in the streets,
    And the complexion of the element
    In favor's like the work we have in hand,
    Most bloody, fiery, and most terrible.   135

Enter CINNA

CASCA Stand close awhile, for here comes one in haste.
CASSIUS 'Tis Cinna, I do know him by his gait;
    He is a friend. Cinna, where haste you so?

Begin it with slender straws. What trash is Rome,

What rubbish, and what garbage, when it serves

Only to provide kindling to illuminate

So vile a being as Caesar! But, oh grief!   115

Where have you led me? Perhaps I say this

Before a willing prisoner; then I know

I'll have to answer for my words. But I am ready,

And dangers are of no concern to me.

CASCA You are speaking to Casca, a man   120

Who is no sneering tattletale. Here, my hand.

Gather a party to remedy these grievances,

And I will be as deeply involved

As any man.

CASSIUS Then we are agreed.   125

Now, Casca, I can tell you that I have already

Enlisted several of the noblest-minded Romans

To undertake with me an effort

Whose effect is both honorable and dangerous.

And I know that at this time, they wait for me   130

On the porch outside Pompey's theatre; now, the night's so bad,

There is no one about walking the streets,

And the character of the sky

Looks just like the work we have in hand,

Very bloody, fiery, and most terrible.   135

Enter CINNA

CASCA Stay out of sight. Here comes someone in a hurry.

CASSIUS It's Cinna. I can tell by his walk.

He is a friend. Cinna, what's your hurry?

CINNA To find you out. Who's that? Metellus Cimber?

CASSIUS Not, it is Casca, one incorporate   140

    To our attempts. Am I not stayed for, Cinna?

CINNA I am glad on't. What a fearful night is this!

    There's two or three of us have seen strange sights.

CASSIUS Am I not stayed for? Tell me.

CINNA Yes, you are.   145

    O Cassius, if you could

    But win the noble Brutus to our party—

CASSIUS Be you content. Good Cinna, take this paper,

    And look you lay it in the praetor's chair,

    Where Brutus may but find it. And throw this   150

    In at his window. Set this up with wax

    Upon old Brutus' statue. All this done,

    Repair to Pompey's porch, where you shall find us.

    Is Decius Brutus and Trebonius there?

CINNA All but Metellus Cimber, and he's gone   155

    To seek you at your house. Well, I will hie,

    And so bestow these papers as you bade me.

CASSIUS That done, repair to Pompey's theatre.

                               Exit CINNA

    Come, Casca, you and I will yet ere day

    See Brutus at his house. Three parts of him   160

    Is ours already, and the man entire

    Upon the next encounter yields him ours.

CASCA O, he sits high in all the people's hearts;

    And that which would appear offense in us

    His countenance, like richest alchemy,   165

CINNA To find you. Who's that? Metellus Cimber?

CASSIUS No, it is Casca who has joined us   140

    In our action. Are they waiting for me, Cinna?

CINNA Glad to hear it. What an awful night this is!

    Two or three of us have seen some strange sights.

CASSIUS Are they still waiting for me? Tell me.

CINNA Yes, they are.   145

    Oh, Cassius, if only you could

    Win the noble Brutus to our cause—

CASSIUS Set your mind at rest. Good Cinna, take this paper,

    And make sure you put it in the magistrate's chair,

    Where only Brutus may find it. And throw this   150

    Through his window. Stick this up with wax

    On the statue of Brutus' ancestor. When you've done this,

    Make your way to Pompey's porch, where you shall find us.

    Are Decius Brutus and Trebonius there?

CINNA Everyone but Metellus Cimber, and he's gone   155

    To seek you at your house. Well, I will hasten

    And distribute these papers as you asked me.

CASSIUS When you're done, make your way to Pompey's theatre.

Exit CINNA

    Come, Casca, you and I before dawn

    Will see Brutus at his house. Three parts of him   160

    We've already won, and the whole man

    On the next meeting will be ours.

CASCA Oh, he sits high in all the people's hearts:

    And what would appear a crime for us to do,

    With his approval, like alchemy,   165

Will change to virtue and to worthiness.

CASSIUS Him and his worth and our great need of him

You have right well conceited. Let us go,

For it is after midnight, and ere day

We will awake him and be sure of him.   170

Exeunt

Would be transformed to virtue and to justice.

CASSIUS Brutus and his prestige and our great need of both,

You have understood and aptly expressed. Let us go,

For it is after midnight, and before dawn

We must wake him and be sure he's with us.   170

Exit

Act Two

Scene 1 [*The garden of Brutus' home.*] *Enter* BRUTUS

BRUTUS What, Lucius, ho!

    I cannot by the progress of the stars

    Give guess how near to day. Lucius, I say!

    I would it were my fault to sleep so soundly.

    When, Lucius, when? Awake, I say! What, Lucius!   5

LUCIUS Called you, my lord?

BRUTUS Get me a taper in my study, Lucius.

    When it is lighted, come and call me here.

LUCIUS I will, my lord.

BRUTUS It must be by his death; and, for my part,   10

    I know of no personal cause to spurn him,

    But for the general. He would be crowned.

    How that might change his nature, there's the question.

    It is the bright day that brings forth the adder,

    And that craves wary walking. Crown him that,   15

    And then, I grant, we put a sting in him

    That at his will he may do danger with.

    Th' abuse of greatness is when it disjoins

    Remorse from power. And, to speak truth of Caesar,

Act Two

Scene 1 [*The garden of Brutus' home.*] *Enter* BRUTUS

BRUTUS   Oh, Lucius, hey there!

    I cannot see the stars to tell

    How near to dawn it is. Lucius, I say!

    I wish it were my fault to sleep so soundly.

    When are you coming, Lucius? Awake, I say. Hey Lucius!   5

LUCIUS   Did you call, my lord?

BRUTUS   Put a candle in my study, Lucius.

    When it is lighted, come and call me here.

LUCIUS   I will, my lord.

BRUTUS   Caesar must die. For my part,   10

    I have no personal reason to strike at him;

    It must be for the general good. He wishes to be crowned.

    How this might alter his nature, that's the point.

    It is the sun that makes the vipers hatch,

    And calls for careful walking. Give Caesar a crown,   15

    And then, I grant, we put a sting in him

    So that, whenever he wishes, he may harm us.

    Authority is abused when it separates

    Power from compassion; and, to be frank about Caesar,

I have not known when his affections swayed   20
More than his reason. But 'tis a common proof
That lowliness is young ambition's ladder,
Whereto the climber-upward turns his face;
But, when he once attains the upmost round,
He then unto the ladder turns his back,   25
Looks in the clouds, scorning the base degrees
By which he did ascend. So Caesar may.
Then, lest he may, prevent. And since the quarrel
Will bear no color for the thing he is,
Fashion it thus: that what he is, augmented,   30
Would run to these and these extremities.
And therefore think of him as a serpent's egg,
Which hatched, would, as his kind, grow mischievous,
And kill him in the shell.

Enter LUCIUS

LUCIUS The taper burneth in your closet, sir.   35
Searching the window for a flint, I found
This paper, thus sealed up, and I am sure
It did not lie there when I went to bed. [*Gives him the letter*]
BRUTUS Get you to bed again; it is not day.
Is not tomorrow, boy, the ides of March?   40
LUCIUS I know not, sir.
BRUTUS Look in the calendar, and bring me word.
LUCIUS I will, sir.

He exits

BRUTUS The exhalations whizzing in the air
Give so much light that I may read by them.   45

48

I have not known a time when passions ruled him   20
More than reason. But everyone knows
That humility is young ambition's ladder,
The upward climber's first rung to power,
And once he's reached the topmost rung,
He turns his back on the ladder,   25
His head in the clouds, scorning the lower steps
By which he rose. Caesar may do the same.
Since he may, he must be stopped. And since the charge
Against him cannot be justified by his present actions,
It must be framed this way: If his present power is increased,   30
It would lead to such and such tyrannical excesses.
Therefore, he must be thought of as a serpent's egg:
Hatched, it would, like all its kind, grow dangerous.
He must be killed in the shell.

Enter LUCIUS

LUCIUS The candle is burning in your study, sir.   35
Searching the ledge for a flint to light it, I found
This letter, sealed up like this, and I am sure
It was not there when I went to bed. [*Gives him the letter*]
BRUTUS Go back to bed; it's not yet day.
Isn't tomorrow the ides of March, boy?   40
LUCIUS I don't know, sir.
BRUTUS Look in the calendar, and come tell me.
LUCIUS I will, sir.

He exits

BRUTUS The meteors hissing in the sky
Give so much light that I can read by it.   45

[*He opens the letter and reads*]

"Brutus, thou sleep'st. Awake, and see thyself!

Shall Rome, *et cetera.* Speak, strike, redress!"

"Brutus, thou sleep'st. Awake!"

Such instigations have often dropped

Where I have took them up.   50

"Shall Rome, *et cetera.*" Thus must I piece out:

Shall Rome stand under one man's awe? What, Rome?

My ancestors did from the streets of Rome

The Tarquin drive, when he was called a king.

"Speak, strike, redress!" Am I entreated   55

To speak and strike? O Rome, I make thee promise,

If the redress will follow, thou receivest

Thy full petition at the hand of Brutus.

       Enter LUCIUS

LUCIUS Sir, March is wasted fifteen days.

Knock within.

BRUTUS 'Tis good. Go to the gate; somebody knocks.   60

       Exit LUCIUS

Since Cassius first did whet me against Caesar

I have not slept.

Between the acting of a dreadful thing

And the first motion, all the interim is

Like a phantasma or a hideous dream.   65

The genius and the mortal instruments

Are then in council, and the state of man,

Like to a little kingdom, suffers then

The nature of an insurrection.

[*He opens the letter and reads*]

"Brutus, you're asleep. Awake and see yourself!

Shall Rome, *et cetera*. Speak, strike, set right!"

"Brutus, you're asleep. Awake!"

Similar incitements have often been dropped

Where I should find them.   50

"Shall Rome, *et cetera*." I must fill in the gaps:

Shall Rome stand in awe of one man? What, Rome?

My ancestors drove from the streets of Rome

The Tarquin when he called himself a king.

"Speak, strike, set right!" Am I begged   55

To speak out and to act? Oh Rome, I make you this promise,

If setting things right will follow, you will receive

All that you request from the hand of Brutus.

Enter LUCIUS

LUCIUS   Sir, it is the fifteenth of March.

Knocking within.

BRUTUS   That's good. Go to the door. Someone is knocking.   60

Exit LUCIUS

Since Cassius first incited me against Caesar,

I have not slept.

From the impulse to a dreadful deed

Till its acting out, all the time between is

Like a nightmare or a hideous dream.   65

The soul and the body that must carry out the action

Engage in a debate, and the human realm,

Like a little kingdom, suffers from

A state of civil war.

Enter LUCIUS

LUCIUS Sir, 'tis your brother Cassius at the door,   70
    Who doth desire to see you.

BRUTUS Is he alone?

LUCIUS No, sir, there are more with him.

BRUTUS Do you know them?

LUCIUS No, sir, their hats are plucked about their ears,   75
    And half their faces buried in their cloaks,
    That by no means I may discover them
    By any mark of favor.

BRUTUS Let 'em enter.

Exit LUCIUS

    They are the faction. O conspiracy,   80
    Sham'st thou to show thy dang'rous brow by night,
    When evils are most free? O, then by day
    Where wilt thou find a cavern dark enough
    To mask thy monstrous visage? Seek none, conspiracy;
    Hide it in smiles and affability;   85
    For if thou path, thy native semblance on,
    Not Erebus itself were dim enough
    To hide thee from prevention.

Enter the conspirators, CASSIUS, CASCA, DECIUS, CINNA, METELLUS
CIMBER, *and* TREBONIUS

CASSIUS I think we are too bold upon your rest.
    Good morrow, Brutus. Do we trouble you?   90

BRUTUS I have been up this hour, awake all night.
    Know I these men that come along with you?

CASSIUS Yes, every man of them; and no man here
    But honors you; and every one doth wish

Enter LUCIUS

LUCIUS Sir, it's your brother-in-law Cassius at the door,   70

    And he wants to see you.

BRUTUS Is he alone?

LUCIUS No, sir, there are more with him.

BRUTUS Do you know them?

CASSIUS No, sir, their hats are pulled over their ears,   75

    And half their faces are buried in their cloaks,

    So there's no way I can tell who they are

    By any of their features.

BRUTUS Let them come in.

Exit LUCIUS

    They are the conspirators. Oh, conspiracy,   80

    Are you ashamed to show your dangerous looks by night,

    When evil can move freely abroad? Oh, then where

    In daytime will you find a cavern dark enough

    To mask your frightful face? Seek none, conspiracy!

    Hide behind smiles and affability.   85

    For if you go about without disguise,

    Not even Erebus itself were dark enough

    To hide you from detection.

Enter the conspirators, CASSIUS, CASCA, DECIUS, CINNA, METELLUS

CIMBER, *and* TREBONIUS

CASSIUS I feel we intrude on you and disturb your sleep.

    Good morning, Brutus. Did we disturb you?   90

BRUTUS I have been up an hour and awake all night.

    Do I know these men who've come along with you?

CASSIUS Yes, every one of them, and none here

    But holds you in honor and wishes

You had but that opinion of yourself   95

Which every noble Roman bears of you.

This is Trebonius.

BRUTUS   He is welcome hither.

CASSIUS   This, Decius Brutus.

BRUTUS   He is welcome too.   100

CASSIUS   This, Casca; this, Cinna; and this, Metellus Cimber.

BRUTUS   They are all welcome.

What watchful cares do interpose themselves

Betwixt your eyes and night?

CASSIUS   Shall I entreat a word?   105

[BRUTUS *and* CASSIUS *whisper aside*]

DECIUS   Here lies the east. Doth not the day break here?

CASCA   No.

CINNA   O, pardon, sir, it doth; and yon grey lines

That fret the clouds are messengers of day.

CASCA   You shall confess that you are both deceived.   110

Here, as I point my sword, the sun arises,

Which is a great way growing on the south,

Weighing the youthful season of the year.

Some two months hence, up higher toward the north

He first presents his fire, and the high east   115

Stands as the Capitol, directly here.

BRUTUS   [*Coming forward*] Give me your hands all over, one by one.

CASSIUS   And let us swear our resolution.

BRUTUS   No, not an oath. If not the face of men,

The sufferance of our souls, the time's abuse—   120

If these be motives weak, break off betimes,

And every man hence to his idle bed.

You had that same opinion of yourself   95

That every noble Roman has of you.

This is Trebonius.

BRUTUS   He is welcome here.

CASSIUS   This, Decius Brutus.

BRUTUS   He is welcome too.   100

CASSIUS   This, Casca. This, Cinna. This, Metellus Cimber.

BRUTUS   They are all welcome.

What worries have kept you awake

And hindered your eyes from closing?

CASSIUS [*to* BRUTUS] A word with you in private.   105

[BRUTUS *and* CASSIUS *whisper aside*]

DECIUS   There's the east. Doesn't day break there?

CASCA   No.

CINNA   Excuse me, sir, but it does. Those gray lines

That lace the clouds are messengers of day.

CASCA   You'll have to admit that you are both mistaken.   110

Here, where I point my sword, the sun rises,

Which is a considerable distance to the south,

Considering that it is still early in the year.

Some two months from now, the sun will rise

Up higher in the north. And due east   115

Stands towards the Capitol, directly here.

BRUTUS [*Coming forward*] Give me your hands, each of you.

CASSIUS   And let us swear our determination.

BRUTUS   No, not an oath. If not the looks on men's faces,

The suffering we feel ourselves, the evils of the time—   120

If these are only weak motives, let's break off at once,

And each man can go back to his empty bed.

So let high-sighted tyranny range on
Till each man drop by lottery. But if these—
As I am sure they do—bear fire enough   125
To kindle cowards and to steel with valor
The melting spirits of women, then, countrymen,
What need we any spur but our own cause
To prick us to redress? What other bond
Than secret Romans that have spoke the word   130
And will not palter? And what other oath
Than honesty to honesty engaged,
That this shall be, or we will fall for it?
Swear priests, and cowards, and men cautelous,
Old feeble carrions, and such suffering souls   135
That welcome wrongs; unto bad causes swear
Such creatures as men doubt; but do not stain
The even virtue of our enterprise,
Nor th' insuppressive mettle of our spirits,
To think that or our cause or our performance   140
Did need an oath, when every drop of blood
That every Roman bears, and nobly bears,
Is guilty of a several bastardy
If he do break the smallest particle
Of any promise that hath passed from him.   145
CASSIUS But what of Cicero? Shall we sound him?
    I think he will stand very strong with us.
CASCA Let us not leave him out.
CINNA No, by no means.

So let tyranny, from its great height, roam

And pick off each man by whim. But if these motives—

As I am sure they do—have sparks enough   125

To fire cowards and steel with valor

The melting spirits of women, then, countrymen,

What need have we of any spur but our own cause

To move us to set things right? What other bond

Than that of cautious Romans who have given their word   130

And will not falter? And what other oath

Than the word of one honest man to another

That this shall take place, or we will die for it?

Make priests swear, as well as cowards and crafty men

And feeble graybeards and submissive men   135

Who welcome injury; men who can't be trusted

Are sworn to evil causes; but do not stain

The flawless virtue of our enterprise

Nor the indomitable quality of our spirit

To think our cause or how we carry it out   140

Needs an oath. Every drop of blood

That every Roman carries, and nobly carries,

Would be adulterated,

If he breaks the smallest part

Of any promise that he has made.   145

CASSIUS But what of Cicero? Shall we sound him out?

    I think he will stand very strong with us.

CASCA Let us not leave him out.

CINNA No, by no means.

METELLUS O, let us have him, for his silver hairs   150
　　Will purchase us a good opinion,
　　And buy men's voices to commend our deeds.
　　It shall be said that his judgment ruled our hands.
　　Our youths and wildness shall no whit appear,
　　But all be buried in his gravity.   155
BRUTUS O, name him not. Let us not break with him,
　　For he will never follow anything
　　That other men begin.
CASSIUS Then leave him out.
CASCA Indeed, he is not fit.   160
DECIUS Shall no man else be touched but only Caesar?
CASSIUS Decius, well urged. I think it is not meet
　　Mark Antony, so well beloved of Caesar,
　　Should outlive Caesar. We shall find of him
　　A shrewd contriver; and, you know, his means,   165
　　If he improve them, may well stretch so far
　　As to annoy us all; which to prevent,
　　Let Antony and Caesar fall together.
BRUTUS Our course will seem too bloody, Caius Cassius,
　　To cut the head off and then hack the limbs,   170
　　Like wrath in death and envy afterwards;
　　For Antony is but a limb of Caesar.
　　Let us be sacrificers, but not butchers, Caius.
　　We all stand up against the spirit of Caesar,
　　And in the spirit of men there is no blood.   175
　　O, that we could then come by Caesar's spirit
　　And not dismember Caesar! But, alas,

METELLUS Oh, let us have him on our side. His silver hairs   150
    Will purchase us a good reputation
    And buy support for our actions.
    It shall be said that his judgment ruled our hands.
    Our youth and wildness shall be noticed not at all,
    But be buried in his dignity.   155

BRUTUS Oh, don't think of him. Let us not approach him,
    For he will never follow anything
    That other men begin.

CASSIUS Then leave him out.

CASCA Indeed, he is not fit.   160

DECIUS Is Caesar our only target, no other man?

CASSIUS A good suggestion, Decius. I think it's not fair
    That Mark Antony, so well beloved of Caesar,
    Should outlive Caesar. We shall find him
    A cunning plotter; and you know, his abilities,   165
    If he makes the most of them, will go so far
    As to harm us all. To prevent this,
    Let Antony and Caesar die together.

BRUTUS Our plan will seem too bloody, Caius Cassius,
    We cut off the head and then hack the limbs,   170
    Seem to kill Caesar in anger and then vent malice on his friends,
    For Antony is only a branch of Caesar.
    Let us be sacrificers, but not butchers, Caius.
    We stand up against the spirit of Caesar,
    And in the spirit of men, there is no blood.   175
    Oh, that we could seize the spirit of Caesar
    And not harm the body! But, alas,

Caesar must bleed for it. And, gentle friends,
Let's kill him boldly, but not wrathfully;
Let's carve him as a dish fit for the gods,   180
Not hew him as a carcass fit for hounds.
And let our hearts, as subtle masters do,
Stir up their servants to an act of rage
And after seem to chide 'em. This shall make
Our purpose necessary, and not envious;   185
Which so appearing to the common eyes,
We shall be called purgers, not murderers.
And for Mark Antony, think not of him,
For he can do no more than Caesar's arm
When Caesar's head is off.   190
CASSIUS   Yet I fear him,
    For in the engrafted love he bears to Caesar—
BRUTUS   Alas, good Cassius, do not think of him.
    If he love Caesar, all that he can do
    Is to himself—take thought, and die for Caesar.   195
    And that were much he should, for he is given
    To sports, to wildness, and much company.
TREBONIUS   There is no fear in him. Let him not die,
    For he will live and laugh at this hereafter.
Clock strikes.
BRUTUS   Peace! Count the clock.   200
CASSIUS   The clock hath stricken three.
TREBONIUS   'Tis time to part.
CASSIUS   But it is doubtful yet
    Whether Caesar will come forth today or no;

Caesar's body must suffer. So, noble friends,

Let's kill him boldly, but not angrily.

Let's carve him as a dish fit for the gods,   180

Not hack him like a carcass fit for dogs.

Let our hearts, like wily masters who

Incite their servants to acts of rage, guide our hands,

And after, seem to scold them. This will prove

Our plan was necessary, and not malicious.   185

We will then be seen in the eyes of the people

As surgeons offering a cure, not murderers.

As for Mark Antony, don't worry about him,

For he can do no more harm than Caesar's arm

When Caesar's head is cut off.   190

CASSIUS Still I fear him,

For the deep-rooted love he bears Caesar—

BRUTUS Really, good Cassius, forget about him.

If he loves Caesar, the only harm he can do

Is to himself—take it to heart and kill himself.   195

And that would be much to expect from him, for he loves

Sports, fast living, and plenty of company.

TREBONIUS There is nothing to fear from him. Let him not be killed.

He'll live to laugh about this later on.

Clock strikes.

BRUTUS Hush. Listen to the time.   200

CASSIUS The clock has struck three.

TREBONIUS It's time to go.

CASSIUS But it is still doubtful

Whether Caesar will appear in public or not;

For he is superstitious grown of late, 205
Quite from the main opinion he held once
Of fantasy, of dreams, and ceremonies.
It may be these apparent prodigies,
The unaccustomed terror of this night,
And the persuasion of his augurers 210
May hold him from the Capitol today.

DECIUS Never fear that. If he be so resolved,
I can o'ersway him; for he loves to hear
That unicorns may be betrayed with trees,
And bears with glasses, elephants with holes, 215
Lions with toils, and men with flatterers.
But when I tell him he hates flatterers,
He says he does, being then most flattered.
Let me work,
For I can give his humor the true bent, 220
And I will bring him to the Capitol.

CASSIUS Nay, we will all of us be there to fetch him.

BRUTUS By the eighth hour, is that the uttermost?

CINNA Be that the uttermost, and fail not then.

METELLUS Caius Ligarius doth bear Caesar hard, 225
Who rated him for speaking well of Pompey.
I wonder none of you have thought of him.

BRUTUS Now, good Metellus, go along by him.
He loves me well, and I have given him reasons.
Send him but hither and I'll fashion him. 230

CASSIUS The morning comes upon 's. We'll leave you, Brutus.
And, friends, disperse yourselves—but all remember

For lately he's grown very superstitious,   205
    Quite contrary to the strong opinion he once held
    Of illusions, dreams, and predictions.
    It may be these wonders that have appeared,
    The unusual terrors of tonight,
    And the influence of his fortune-tellers,   210
    Will keep him from the Capitol today.

DECIUS Don't worry about that. If that's what he intends,
    I'll persuade him otherwise. He loves to hear
    How unicorns are tricked to run into tree trunks,
    Bears fooled by mirrors, elephants fall into pits,   215
    Lions caught with snares, and men fooled by flatterers.
    And when I tell him he hates flatterers,
    He says he does, unaware he's being flattered.
    Let me work on him,
    For I can shape his mood the right way,   220
    And I will bring him to the Capitol.

CASSIUS No, we'll all be there to fetch him.

BRUTUS By eight o'clock, at the latest?

CINNA That's the latest; don't miss the time.

METELLUS Caius Ligarius hates Caesar,   225
    Who berated him for speaking well of Pompey.
    I wonder why none of you thought of him.

BRUTUS Well, good Metellus, stop by his house.
    He likes me very much and owes me some favors.
    Send him here, and I'll persuade him.   230

CASSIUS It's nearly morning. We'll leave you Brutus.
    And, friends, scatter—but all remember

What you have said, and show yourselves true Romans.

BRUTUS Good gentlemen, look fresh and merrily.

Let not our looks put on our purposes,   235

But bear it as our Roman actors do,

With untired spirits and formal constancy.

And so good morrow to you every one.

Exeunt all but BRUTUS

Boy! Lucius! Fast asleep? It is no matter.

Enjoy the honey-heavy dew of slumber,   240

Thou hast no figures, nor no fantasies,

Which busy care draws in the brains of men.

Therefore thou sleep'st so sound.

Enter PORTIA

PORTIA Brutus, my lord.

BRUTUS Portia! What mean you? Wherefore rise you now?   245

It is not for your health thus to commit

Your weak condition to the raw cold morning.

PORTIA Nor for yours neither. Y' have ungently, Brutus,

Stole from my bed; and yesternight at supper

You suddenly arose and walked about,   250

Musing and sighing, with your arms across,

And when I asked you what the matter was,

You stared upon me with ungentle looks.

I urged you further, then you scratched your head

And too impatiently stamped with your foot.   255

Yet I insisted, yet you answered not,

But with an angry wafture of your hand

Gave sign for me to leave you. So I did,

What you have said and show yourselves as true Romans.

BRUTUS Good gentlemen, look bright and cheerful,

    Don't let our faces reveal our intentions,   235

    But look the way our Roman actors do,

    With resolution and formal composure.

    And so, good morning to you, everyone.

Exit all but BRUTUS

    Boy! Lucius! Fast asleep? It doesn't matter,

    Enjoy the honey-heavy dew of slumber.   240

    You have no imaginings nor illusions

    That restless care conjures up in the minds of men;

    And so you sleep soundly.

Enter PORTIA

PORTIA Brutus, my lord.

BRUTUS Portia, what do you want? Why are you up now?   245

    It is not good for your health to expose

    Your delicate constitution to the raw, cold morning.

PORTIA Nor for yours, either. You have rudely, Brutus,

    Stolen from my bed; and last night at supper,

    You suddenly arose and walked about,   250

    Thinking and sighing, with your arms crossed,

    And when I asked you what the matter was,

    You stared at me with angry looks.

    I asked you again, then you scratched your head

    And irritably stamped your foot.   255

    Still I insisted, and you did not answer me,

    But with an angry wave of your hand,

    Signalled me to leave you. So I did,

Fearing to strengthen that impatience
Which seemed too much enkindled, and withal 260
Hoping it was but an effect of humor
Which sometime hath his hour with every man.
It will not let you eat nor talk nor sleep;
And could it work so much upon your shape
As it hath much prevailed on your condition, 265
I should not know you, Brutus. Dear my lord,
Make me acquainted with your cause of grief.

BRUTUS   I am not well in health, and that is all.

PORTIA   Brutus is wise, and were he not in health,
He would embrace the means to come by it. 270

BRUTUS   Why, so I do. Good Portia, go to bed.

PORTIA   Is Brutus sick? And is it physical
To walk unbraced and suck up the humors
Of the dank morning? What, is Brutus sick
And he will steal out of his wholesome bed 275
To dare the vile contagion of the night
And tempt the rheumy and unpurged air
To add unto his sickness? No, my Brutus,
You have some sick offense within your mind,
Which by the right and virtue of my place 280
I ought to know of. And upon my knees
I charm you, by my once commended beauty,
By all your vows of love, and that great vow
Which did incorporate and make us one,
That you unfold to me, your self, your half, 285
Why you are heavy, and what men tonight

Fearing to worsen that impatience

That already seemed excessive, and after all   260

Hoping it was only the effect of some passing mood,

From which every man from time to time suffers.

It will not let you eat or talk or sleep;

And if it could change your appearance

As much as it has influenced your state of mind,   265

I should not know you, Brutus. My dear,

Tell me the cause of your distress.

BRUTUS I am not well. That's all.

PORTIA Brutus is sensible. If his health were poor,

    He would adopt the means to restore it.   270

BRUTUS Why, so I do. Good Portia, go back to bed.

PORTIA If Brutus is sick, is it healthy for him

    To walk about with clothes unfastened and breathe

    The damp morning air? What, is Brutus sick?

    And does he creep out of his healthful bed   275

    To risk the diseases carried in the night air,

    Tempting this infectious sunless air

    To add to his sickness? No, my Brutus,

    You have some sickness in your mind,

    Which, because I am your wife,   280

    I ought to know. And upon my knees

    I implore you, by my once praised beauty,

    By all your vows of love, and by that great vow

    That made us man and wife,

    That you reveal to me, your other half, a part of yourself,   285

    Why you are so sad and who those men were tonight

Have had resort to you, for here have been
Some six or seven who did hide their faces
Even from the darkness.

BRUTUS Kneel not, gentle Portia.   290

PORTIA I should not need if you were gentle, Brutus.
Within the bond of marriage, tell me, Brutus,
Is it excepted I should know no secrets
That appertain to you? Am I your self
But, as it were, in sort or limitation,   295
To keep with you at your meals, comfort your bed,
And talk to you sometimes? Dwell I but in the suburbs
Of your good pleasure? If it be no more
Portia is Brutus' harlot, not his wife.

BRUTUS You are my true and honorable wife,   300
As dear to me as are the ruddy drops
That visit my sad heart.

PORTIA If this were true, then I should know this secret.
I grant I am a woman, but withal
A woman that Lord Brutus took to wife.   305
I grant I am a woman, but withal
A woman well reputed, Cato's daughter.
Think you I am no stronger than my sex,
Being so fathered and so husbanded?
Tell me your counsels; I will not disclose 'em.   310
I have made strong proof of my constancy,
Giving myself a voluntary wound
Here, in the thigh. Can I bear that with patience
And not my husband's secrets?

Who visited you; for there have been

Some six or seven men who hid their faces

Even from the dark night.

BRUTUS Do not kneel, gentle Portia.   290

PORTIA I would not need to, if you were gentle, Brutus.

Tell me, Brutus, is it an exception

To our marriage bond that I should know no secrets

That have reference to you? Am I part of you

But, as it were, only in a certain way and for a certain time,   295

To sit with you at meals, to gladden your bed,

And talk to you occasionally? Is my place in the outskirts

Of your affection? If it is no more,

Portia is Brutus' mistress, not his wife.

BRUTUS You are my true and honorable wife,   300

As dear to me as the red blood

Of my sad heart.

PORTIA If that were true, then I should know this secret.

I grant I am a woman, but all the same

The woman that Lord Brutus took as his wife.   305

I grant I am a woman, but all the same

A woman of good family, Cato's daughter.

Do you think that I am like any other woman,

With such a father and such a husband?

Tell me your secret thoughts; I'll not disclose them.   310

I have made a strong test of my fortitude,

I have slashed myself deliberately

Here, in the thigh. Could I bear this with patience

And not my husband's secrets?

BRUTUS O ye gods,

    Render me worthy of this noble wife!   315

Knocking.

    Hark, hark, one knocks. Portia, go in a while,

    And by and by thy bosom shall partake

    The secrets of my heart.

    All my engagements I will construe to thee,

    All the charactery of my sad brows.   320

    Leave me with haste.

                                Exit PORTIA

    Lucius, who's that knocks?

               Enter LUCIUS *and* LIGARIUS

LUCIUS Here is a sick man that would speak with you.

BRUTUS Caius Ligarius, that Metellus spake of.

    Boy, stand aside.   325

                                Exit LUCIUS

    Caius Ligarius, how?

LIGARIUS Vouchsafe good morrow from a feeble tongue.

BRUTUS O, what a time have you chose out, brave Caius,

    To wear a kerchief! Would you were not sick!

LIGARIUS I am not sick if Brutus have in hand   330

    Any exploit worthy the name of honor.

BRUTUS Such an exploit have I in hand, Ligarius,

    Had you a healthful ear to hear of it.

LIGARIUS By all the gods that Romans bow before,

    I here discard my sickness! [*He throws off his kerchief*]   335

    Soul of Rome,

    Brave son, derived from honorable loins,

BRUTUS Oh, you gods,

    Make me worthy of this noble wife!   315

Knocking.

    Wait, wait. Someone knocks. Portia, go inside awhile.

    By and by your heart shall share

    The secrets of my heart.

    All my commitments I will explain to you,

    All that is written on my sad brow.   320

    Leave me, quickly.

                       Exit PORTIA

    Lucius, who's knocking?

          Enter LUCIUS *and* CAIUS LIGARIUS

LUCIUS Here's a sick man who wants to speak to you.

BRUTUS Caius Ligarius. Metellus was talking of you.

    Boy, you may go.   325

                    Exit LUCIUS

    Caius Ligarius, how are you?

LIGARIUS Be so good as to accept my greeting of "good morning."

BRUTUS Oh, what a time you have chosen, noble Caius,

    To be ill. I wish you were not sick.

LIGARIUS I am not sick if Brutus has at hand   330

    A plan worthy to be called honorable.

BRUTUS Such a plan I have in hand, Ligarius,

    If only your ear was healthy enough to hear it.

LIGARIUS By all the gods that Romans bow before,

    I here throw off my sickness.   335

    Soul of Rome,

    Noble son of an honorable father,

Thou like an exorcist has conjured up
My mortified spirit. Now bid me run,
And I will strive with things impossible,   340
Yea, get the better of them. What's to do?

BRUTUS A piece of work that will make sick men whole.

LIGARIUS But are not some whole that we must make sick?

BRUTUS That must we also. What it is, my Caius,
I shall unfold to thee as we are going   345
To whom it must be done.

LIGARIUS Set on your foot,
And with a heart new-fired I follow you,
To do I know not what; but it sufficeth
That Brutus leads me on.   350

Thunder.

BRUTUS Follow me then.

Exeunt

Scene 2 [*Caesar's house. Early morning*]

Thunder and lightning. Enter JULIUS CAESAR *in his nightgown*

CAESAR Nor heaven nor earth have been at peace tonight.
Thrice hath Calpurnia in her sleep cried out,
"Help ho, they murder Caesar!" Who's within?

Enter a SERVANT

SERVANT My lord?

CAESAR Go bid the priests do present sacrifice   5
And bring me their opinions of success.

SERVANT I will, my lord.

Exit SERVANT

72

Like a magician, you have brought

My dead spirits back to life. Ask me to run,

And I will attempt the impossible, 340

Yes, and get the better of it. What's to be done?

BRUTUS A task that will make sick men whole.

LIGARIUS But are not some whole that we must make sick?

BRUTUS That we must also do. What it is, my Caius,

I will explain to you as we go to meet 345

The person to whom it must be done.

LIGARIUS Lead the way,

And with a heart new-fired I will follow you,

To do what I don't know; it's enough

That Brutus leads me. 350

Thunder.

BRUTUS Follow me then.

Exit

Scene 2 [*Caesar's house. Early morning*]

Thunder and lightning. Enter JULIUS CAESAR *in his dressing gown*

CAESAR Neither heaven nor earth has been at peace tonight.

Three times Calpurnia has cried out in her sleep,

"Help here, they are murdering Caesar." Who's there?

Enter a SERVANT

SERVANT My lord?

CAESAR Go ask the priests to make an immediate sacrifice, 5

And bring me the result, good or bad omens.

SERVANT I will, my lord.

Exit SERVANT

Enter CALPURNIA

CALPURNIA What mean you, Caesar? Think you to walk forth?

    You shall not stir out of your house today.

CAESAR Caesar shall forth. The things that threatened me   10

    Ne'er looked but on my back; when they shall see

    The face of Caesar, they are vanished.

CALPURNIA Caesar, I never stood on ceremonies,

    Yet now they fright me. There is one within,

    Besides the things that we have heard and seen,   15

    Recounts most horrid sights seen by the watch.

    A lioness hath whelped in the streets

    And graves have yawned and yielded up their dead.

    Fierce fiery warriors fought upon the clouds

    In ranks and squadrons and right form of war,   20

    Which drizzled blood upon the Capitol.

    The noise of battle hurtled in the air,

    Horses did neigh and dying men did groan,

    And ghosts did shriek and squeal about the streets.

    O Caesar, these things are beyond all use,   25

    And I do fear them.

CAESAR What can be avoided

    Whose end is purposed by the mighty gods?

    Yet Caesar shall go forth, for these predictions

    Are to the world in general as to Caesar.   30

CALPURNIA When beggars die there are no comets seen,

    The heavens themselves blaze forth the death of princes.

CAESAR Cowards die many times before their deaths,

    The valiant never taste of death but once.

Enter CALPURNIA

CALPURNIA What do you intend, Caesar? Are you planning to go out?

You shall not stir out of your house today.

CAESAR Caesar shall go out. The things that threatened me   10

Only looked at my back; when they shall see

The face of Caesar, they have vanished.

CALPURNIA Caesar, I never paid attention to omens,

But now they frighten me. One of our household reports,

Besides the things we have heard and seen,   15

Some horrid sights seen by the night watch.

A lioness gave birth in the streets.

And graves gaped and gave up their dead.

Fierce, fiery warriors fought in the clouds,

In ranks and squadrons, correct battle order,   20

Causing blood to drizzle on the Capitol.

The noises of battle collided in the air.

Horses neighed and dying men groaned.

And ghosts shrieked and squealed in the streets.

Oh, Caesar, these things are beyond all experience,   25

And I fear them.

CAESAR What can be prevented

When it is destined by the mighty gods?

Still, Caesar shall go out, for these predictions

Apply as much to the rest of the world as to Caesar.   30

CALPURNIA When beggars die, no comets are seen,

The heavens themselves blaze forth the death of princes.

CAESAR Cowards die many times before their deaths,

Brave men never taste of death but once.

Of all the wonders that I yet have heard   35

It seems to me most strange that men should fear,

Seeing that death, a necessary end,

Will come when it will come.

Enter a SERVANT

What say the augurers?

SERVANT They would not have you stir forth today.   40

Plucking the entrails of an offering forth,

They could not find a heart within the beast.

CAESAR The gods do this in shame of cowardice.

Caesar should be a beast without a heart

If he should stay at home today for fear.   45

No, Caesar shall not. Danger knows full well

That Caesar is more dangerous than he.

We are two lions littered in one day,

And I the elder and more terrible.

And Caesar shall go forth.   50

CALPURNIA Alas, my lord,

Your wisdom is consumed in confidence.

Do not go forth today. Call it my fear

That keeps you in the house, and not your own.

We'll send Mark Antony to the Senate House   55

And he shall say you are not well today.

Let me, upon my knee, prevail in this.

CAESAR Mark Antony shall say I am not well,

And for thy humor I will stay at home.

Enter DECIUS

Here's Decius Brutus, he shall tell them so.   60

Of all the wonders that I have heard,   35

It seems to me most strange that men fear death,

Seeing that death, which is inevitable,

Will come when it will come.

Enter a SERVANT

What do the fortune tellers have to say?

SERVANT They would not have you go out today.   40

Removing the innards of the sacrifice,

They could not find a heart within the beast.

CAESAR The gods do this to put cowards to shame.

Caesar would be a beast without a heart

If he should stay at home today from fear.   45

No, Caesar shall not. Danger knows full well

That Caesar is more dangerous than he.

We are two lions of the same litter,

And I'm the elder and more terrible.

So Caesar shall go forth.   50

CALPURNIA Alas, my lord,

Your wisdom is eaten up with confidence.

Do not go out today. Say it is my fear

That keeps you in the house, and not your own.

We'll send Mark Antony to the Senate House,   55

And he shall say you are not well today.

Let me, on my knee, have my way in this.

CAESAR Mark Antony shall say I am not well,

And to please you, I'll stay at home.

Enter DECIUS

Here's Decius Brutus. He shall tell them so.   60

DECIUS Caesar, all hail! Good morrow, worthy Caesar.

    I come to fetch you to the Senate House.

CAESAR And you are come in very happy time

    To bear my greetings to the senators

    And tell them that I will not come today.   65

    Cannot is false, and that I dare not, falser.

    I will not come today. Tell them so, Decius.

CALPURNIA Say he is sick.

CAESAR Shall Caesar send a lie?

    Have I in conquest stretched mine arm so far   70

    To be afeard to tell graybeards the truth?

    Decius, go tell them Caesar will not come.

DECIUS Most mighty Caesar, let me know some cause,

    Lest I be laughed at when I tell them so.

CAESAR The cause is my will. I will not come.   75

    That is enough to satisfy the Senate.

    But for your private satisfaction,

    Because I love you, I will let you know.

    Calpurnia here, my wife, stays me at home.

    She dreamt tonight she saw my statue,   80

    Which like a fountain with an hundred spouts

    Did run pure blood, and many lusty Romans

    Came smiling and did bathe their hands in it.

    And these does she apply for warnings and portents

    And evils imminent, and on her knee   85

    Hath begged that I will stay at home today.

DECIUS This dream is all amiss interpreted.

    It was a vision fair and fortunate.

DECIUS Caesar, all hail! Good morning, worthy Caesar.
  I've come to conduct you to the Senate House.

CAESAR You've come at a most opportune moment
  To carry my greetings to the senators
  And tell them that I will not come today.   65
  "Cannot" is untrue; "dare not" is even falser.
  I will not come today. Tell them so, Decius.

CALPURNIA Say that he is sick.

CAESAR Shall Caesar send a lie?
  Have I stretched my arm so far in conquest,   70
  And am now afraid to tell graybeards the truth?
  Decius, go tell them Caesar will not come.

DECIUS Mighty Caesar, let me have a reason,
  Lest I be laughed at when I tell them.

CAESAR The reason is that I will it. I will not come.   75
  That is enough to satisfy the Senate.
  But for your personal information,
  Because I love you, I will let you know this:
  Calpurnia here, my wife, keeps me at home.
  She dreamed last night she saw my statue,   80
  And it was like a fountain with a hundred spouts,
  All running pure blood, and many vigorous Romans
  Came smiling and bathed their hands in it.
  And these she interprets as warnings and omens
  Of imminent evil, and on her knee   85
  Has begged me to stay at home today.

DECIUS This dream was interpreted all incorrectly.
  It is a vision promising good fortune.

Your statue spouting blood in many pipes,
In which so many smiling Romans bathed,   90
Signifies that from you great Rome shall suck
Reviving blood and that great men shall press
For tinctures, stains, relics, and cognizance.
This by Calpurnia's dream is signified.
CAESAR And this way have you well expounded it.   95
DECIUS I have, when you have heard what I can say.
　　And know it now: the Senate have concluded
　　To give this day a crown to mighty Caesar.
　　If you shall send them word you will not come,
　　Their minds may change. Besides, it were a mock   100
　　Apt to be rendered for someone to say,
　　"Break up the Senate till another time,
　　When Caesar's wife shall meet with better dreams."
　　If Caesar hide himself, shall they not whisper,
　　"Lo, Caesar is afraid"?   105
　　Pardon me, Caesar, for my dear dear love
　　To your proceeding bids me tell you this,
　　And reason to my love is liable.
CAESAR How foolish do your fears seem now, Calpurnia!
　　I am ashamed I did yield to them.   110
　　Give me my robe, for I will go.
　　Enter BRUTUS, LIGARIUS, METELLUS, CASCA, TREBONIUS, CINNA, *and*
　　　　　　　　　　　　　　　PUBLIUS
　　And look where Publius is come to fetch me.
PUBLIUS Good morrow, Caesar.
CAESAR Welcome, Publius.

Your statue spouting blood from many pipes,

In which so many smiling Romans bathed, 90

Means that from you great Rome draws

Its lifeblood, and that great men look to you

For sacred tokens and recognition of nobility.

This is what Calpurnia's dream means.

CAESAR And in this way you have well explained it. 95

DECIUS I have. You shall hear what I have to say

And know it now: the Senate had decided

To give to mighty Caesar a crown today.

If you send word that you will not come,

Their minds may change. Besides, 100

Someone is apt to mockingly joke,

"Let's adjourn the Senate till another time,

When Caesar's wife shall have better dreams."

If Caesar hides himself, won't people whisper,

"Look, Caesar is afraid"? 105

Pardon me, Caesar, it is my dear dear concern

For your advancement that leads me to tell you this.

Prudence is overcome by my love.

CAESAR How foolish your fears seem now, Calpurnia!

I am ashamed I gave in to them. 110

Give me my robe, for I will go.

Enter BRUTUS, LIGARIUS, METELLUS, CASCA, TREBONIUS, CINNA, *and*

PUBLIUS

And look, here's Publius come to fetch me.

PUBLIUS Good morning, Caesar.

CAESAR Welcome, Publius.

What, Brutus, are you stirred so early too? 115

Good morrow, Casca. Caius Ligarius,

Caesar was ne'er so much your enemy

As that same ague which hath made you lean.

What is 't o'clock?

BRUTUS Caesar, 'tis strucken eight. 120

CAESAR I thank you for your pains and courtesy.

Enter ANTONY

See, Antony, that revels long a-nights,

Is notwithstanding up. Good morrow, Antony.

ANTONY So to most noble Caesar.

CAESAR [*to* CALPURNIA] Bid them prepare within, 125

Exit CALPURNIA

I am to blame to be thus waited for.

Now, Cinna, now, Metellus. What, Trebonius,

I have an hour's talk in store for you.

Remember that you call on me today;

Be near me that I may remember you. 130

TREBONIUS Caesar, I will. [*Aside*] And so near will I be

That your best friends shall wish I had been further.

CAESAR Good friends, go in and taste some wine with me,

And we, like friends, will straightway go together.

BRUTUS [*Aside*] That every like is not the same, O Caesar, 135

The heart of Brutus earns to think upon.

Exeunt

What, Brutus, are you up early too? 115

Good morning, Casca. Caius Ligarius,

Caesar was never so great an enemy

As that illness which has made you thin.

What time is it?

BRUTUS Caesar, the clock's struck eight. 120

CAESAR Thank you for your trouble.

Enter ANTONY

See, even Antony, the late-reveler

Is also up. Good morning, Antony.

ANTONY And to you, noble Caesar.

CAESAR [*to* CALPURNIA] Bid them to make preparations inside. 125

Exit CALPURNIA

I am to blame for keeping you waiting.

Well, Cinna. How are you, Metellus? What, Trebonius?

I have an hour's talk in store for you.

Remember to call on me today,

And stay close so that I may remember you. 130

TREBONIUS Caesar, I will. [*Aside*] And I'll be so close

That your best friends will wish I had been farther away.

CAESAR Good friends, go in and taste some wine with me.

And we, like friends, will go together right away.

BRUTUS [*Aside*] "Like friends" is not the same as "being friends." 135

Oh, Caesar, the heart of Brutus grieves to think about it.

All exit

Scene 3 [*A street near the Capitol*]

Enter ARTEMIDORUS, *reading a letter*

ARTEMIDORUS "Caesar, beware of Brutus, take heed of Cassius, come not
near Casca, have an eye to Cinna, trust not Trebonius, mark well
Metellus Cimber, Decius Brutus loves thee not, thou hast wronged
Caius Ligarius. There is but one mind in all these men, and it is
bent against Caesar. If thou beest not immortal, look about you.   5
Security gives way to conspiracy. The mighty gods defend thee!

Thy lover,

Artemidorus"

Here will I stand till Caesar pass along,
And as a suitor will I give him this.   10
My heart laments that virtue cannot live
Out of the teeth of emulation.
If thou read this, O Caesar, thou mayest live;
If not, the fates with traitors do conspire.

Exit

Scene 4 [*Outside the house of Brutus*]

Enter PORTIA *and* LUCIUS

PORTIA I prithee, boy, run to the Senate House.
Stay not to answer me but get thee gone.
Why dost thou stay?

LUCIUS To know my errand, madam.

PORTIA I would have had thee there and here again   5
Ere I can tell thee what thou shouldst do there.

Scene 3 [*A street near the Capitol*]

Enter ARTEMIDORUS, *reading a letter*

ARTEMIDORUS "Caesar, beware of Brutus, take heed of Cassius. Stay away
from Casca. Look out for Cinna. Don't trust Trebonius. Keep an eye
on Metellus Cimber. Decius Brutus hates you. You have wronged
Caius Ligarius. These men are all of one mind, and it is turned
against Caesar. If you are not immortal, keep your eyes open. Over-   5
confidence leads the way to conspiracy. The mighty gods defend you!

          Your admirer,

          Artemidorus"

Here will I stand till Caesar passes by,
And as a petitioner I will give him this.   10
My heart laments that virtue cannot live
Beyond reach of envy's fangs.
If you read this, Caesar, you may still live;
If not, the fates conspire to aid traitors.

                           Exit

Scene 4   [*Outside the house of Brutus*]

Enter PORTIA *and* LUCIUS

PORTIA I ask you, boy, run to the Senate House.
Don't wait to answer me. Get going.
Why are you standing there?

LUCIUS To know my errand, madam.

PORTIA I would have had you go and return again   5
Before I could tell you what you should do there.

[*Aside*] O constancy, be strong upon my side,

Set a huge mountain 'tween my heart and tongue!

I have a man's mind, but a woman's might,

How hard it is for women to keep counsel!— 10

Art thou here yet?

LUCIUS Madam, what should I do?

Run to the Capitol, and nothing else?

And so return to you, and nothing else?

PORTIA Yes, bring me word, boy, if thy lord look well, 15

For he went sickly forth, and take good note

What Caesar doth, what suitors press to him.

Hark, boy, what noise is that?

LUCIUS I hear none, madam.

PORTIA Prithee, listen well. 20

I hear a bustling rumor, like a fray,

And the wind brings it from the Capitol.

LUCIUS Sooth, madam, I hear nothing.

Enter the SOOTHSAYER

PORTIA Come hither, fellow, which way hast thou been?

SOOTHSAYER At mine own house, good lady. 25

PORTIA What is 't o'clock?

SOOTHSAYER About the ninth hour, lady.

PORTIA Is Caesar yet gone to the Capitol?

SOOTHSAYER Madam, not yet. I go to take my stand

To see him pass on to the Capitol. 30

PORTIA Thou hast some suit to Caesar, hast thou not?

SOOTHSAYER That I have, lady, if it will please Caesar

To be so good to Caesar as to hear me:

[*Aside*] Oh, fortitude be on my side,

Build a huge mountain between my heart and tongue.

I have a man's mind but the strength of a woman.

How hard it is for women to keep a secret!— 10

Are you still here?

LUCIUS Madam, what do you want me to do?

Run to the Capitol, and nothing else?

And then return to you, and nothing else?

PORTIA Yes, bring me word, boy, if your lord looks well. 15

He looked ill when he left. And take good note

Of what Caesar does, who seek favors from him.

Listen, boy, what was that noise?

LUCIUS I heard no noise, madam.

PORTIA Please, listen well. 20

I hear a confused noise, like fighting,

And the wind brings it from the Capitol.

LUCIUS Honestly, madam, I hear nothing.

Enter the FORTUNE-TELLER

PORTIA Come here, sir, where have you been?

FORTUNE-TELLER At my own house, madam. 25

PORTIA What time is it?

FORTUNE-TELLER About nine, madam.

PORTIA Has Caesar yet gone to the Capitol?

FORTUNE-TELLER Madam, not yet. I am going to find a place

To see him pass on the way to the Capitol. 30

PORTIA You have some petition for Caesar, haven't you?

FORTUNE-TELLER That I have, madam. If it will please Caesar

To be so good as to hear me,

I shall beseech him to befriend himself.

PORTIA Why, know'st thou any harm's intended towards him?   35

SOOTHSAYER None that I know will be, much that I fear may chance.

Good morrow to you. Here the street is narrow.

The throng that follows Caesar at the heels,

Of senators, of praetors, common suitors,

Will crowd a feeble man almost to death.   40

I'll get me to a place more void, and there

Speak to great Caesar as he comes along.

Exit

PORTIA I must go in. [*Aside*] Ay me, how weak a thing

The heart of woman is! O Brutus,

The heavens speed thee in thine enterprise!   45

Sure the boy heard me. [*To* LUCIUS] Brutus hath a suit

That Caesar will not grant. O, I grow faint.

Run, Lucius, and commend me to my lord,

Say I am merry. Come to me again

And bring me word what he doth say to thee.   50

Exeunt

I shall beg Caesar to do himself a favor.

PORTIA Why, do you know that anyone intends to harm him?   35

FORTUNE-TELLER Nothing I know for certain, but much that I fear.

Good morning to you. The street is narrow here.

The throng that follows Caesar at his heel—

The senators, the praetors, the humble petitioners—

Might crowd a feeble man almost to death.   40

I'll find a more open place, and there

Speak to great Caesar as he comes along.

He exits

PORTIA I must go in. [*Aside*] Alas, how weak a thing

Is the heart of woman! Oh, Brutus,

May the heavens help you in your enterprise.   45

I'm sure the boy heard me. [*To* LUCIUS] Brutus has a request

That Caesar will not grant. Oh, I grow faint.

Run, Lucius, and give my lord my love.

Say I am in good spirits. Return

And bring me word what he has said to you.   50

They exit separately

Act Three

Scene 1 *Flourish. Enter* CAESAR, BRUTUS, CASSIUS, CASCA, DECIUS,
METELLUS, TREBONIUS, CINNA, ANTONY, LEPIDUS, POPILIUS, *and*
PUBLIUS. *Among the crowd are* ARTEMIDORUS *and the* SOOTHSAYER

CAESAR The ides of March are come.

SOOTHSAYER Ay, Caesar, but not gone.

ARTEMIDORUS Hail, Caesar! Read this schedule.

DECIUS Trebonius doth desire you to o'erread,

    At your best leisure, this humble suit.   5

ARTEMIDORUS O Caesar, read mine first, for mine's a suit

    That touches Caesar nearer. Read it, great Caesar.

CAESAR What touches us ourself shall last be served.

ARTEMIDORUS Delay not, Caesar, read it instantly.

CAESAR What, is the fellow mad?   10

PUBLIUS Sirrah, give place.

CASSIUS What, urge you your petitions in the street?

    Come to the Capitol.

[*Caesar moves forward, the rest following*]

POPILIUS I wish your enterprise today may thrive.

CASSIUS What enterprise, Popilius?   15

POPILIUS Fare you well.

BRUTUS What said Popilius Lena?

CASSIUS He wished today our enterprise might thrive.

    I fear our purpose is discovered.

BRUTUS Look how he makes to Caesar. Mark him.   20

CASSIUS Casca, be sudden, for we fear prevention.

    Brutus, what shall be done? If this be known,

Act Three

Scene 1 *Trumpet Fanfare. Enter* CAESAR, BRUTUS, CASSIUS, CASCA,
DECIUS, METELLUS, TREBONIUS, CINNA, ANTONY, LEPIDUS, POPILIUS, *and*
PUBLIUS. *Among the crowd are* ARTEMIDORUS *and the* FORTUNE-TELLER

CAESAR The ides of March have come.

FORTUNE-TELLER Yes, Caesar, but not yet passed.

ARTEMIDORUS Hail, Caesar! read this document.

DECIUS Trebonius would like you to read through,

　　When it is convenient, this humble petition.　　　　　　　　　5

ARTEMIDORUS Oh, Caesar, read mine first, for mine's an appeal

　　Of more personal concern to you. Read it, great Caesar.

CAESAR What concerns Caesar personally shall wait till last.

ARTEMIDORUS Don't delay, Caesar, read it immediately.

CAESAR What, is the man mad?　　　　　　　　　　　　　　10

PUBLIUS Sir, get out of the way.

CASSIUS What, are you pushing your petition in the street?

　　Come to the Capitol.

[*Caesar moves forward, the rest following*]

POPILIUS I wish your scheme today may succeed.

CASSIUS What scheme, Popilius?　　　　　　　　　　　　　15

POPILIUS Goodbye, now.

BRUTUS What did Popilius Lena say?

CASSIUS He wished our scheme today might succeed.

　　I fear our plot has been discovered.

BRUTUS Look how he makes his way to Caesar. Watch him.　　20

CASSIUS Casca, be quick. We fear his intervention.

　　Brutus, what shall we do? If we're exposed,

Cassius or Caesar never shall turn back,

For I will slay myself.

BRUTUS Cassius, be constant.   25

Popilius Lena speaks not of our purposes,

For look he smiles, and Caesar doth not change.

CASSIUS Trebonius knows his time, for look you, Brutus,

He draws Mark Antony out of the way.

Exeunt ANTONY *and* TREBONIUS

DECIUS Where is Metellus Cimber? Let him go   30

And presently prefer his suit to Caesar.

BRUTUS He is addressed, press near and second him.

CINNA Casca, you are the first that rears your hand.

CAESAR Are we all ready? What is now amiss

That Caesar and his Senate must redress?   35

METELLUS Most high, most mighty, and most puissant Caesar,

Metellus Cimber throws before thy seat

An humble heart. [*He kneels*]

CAESAR I must prevent thee, Cimber.

These couchings and these lowly courtesies   40

Might fire the blood of ordinary men

And turn preordinance and first decree

Into the law of children. Be not fond

To think that Caesar bears such rebel blood

That will be thawed from the true quality   45

With that which melteth fools—I mean sweet words,

Low-crooked curtsies, and base spaniel fawning.

Thy brother by decree is banished.

If thou dost bend, and pray, and fawn for him,

Cassius or Caesar shall never return alive,

For I will slay myself.

BRUTUS Cassius, control yourself. 25

Popilius Lena is not exposing our plans.

Look how he smiles, and Caesar hasn't changed.

CASSIUS Trebonius knows when to act. Look, Brutus,

He draws Mark Antony out of the way.

Exit ANTONY *and* TREBONIUS

DECIUS Where is Metellus Cimber? Let him go 30

And at once present his petition to Caesar.

BRUTUS He is ready; get near and back him up.

CINNA Casca, you are the first to raise your hand.

CAESAR Are we all ready? What is wrong

That Caesar and his Senate must set right? 35

METELLUS Most high, most mighty, and most powerful Caesar,

Metellus Cimber throws before your throne,

A humble heart. [*He kneels*]

CAESAR I must stop you, Cimber.

All this bowing and grovelling 40

Might inflame the pride of ordinary men

And turn the original and time-honored laws

Into rules for children's games. Don't be so foolish as

To think Caesar is so untrue to his own nature

That he can be thawed from his original firmness 45

By things that melt fools—I mean sweet words,

Low curtsies, and low, spaniel-like fawning.

Your brother has been banished by decree.

If you bow and scrape and pray for him,

I spurn thee like a cur out of my way.   50

Know Caesar doth not wrong, nor without cause

Will he be satisfied.

METELLUS Is there no voice more worthy than my own

To sound more sweetly in great Caesar's ear

For the repealing of my banished brother?   55

BRUTUS I kiss thy hand, but not in flattery, Caesar,

Desiring thee that Publius Cimber may

Have an immediate freedom of repeal.

CAESAR What, Brutus?

CASSIUS Pardon, Caesar! Caesar, pardon!   60

As low as to thy foot doth Cassius fall

To beg enfranchisement for Publius Cimber.

CAESAR I could be well moved, if I were as you.

If I could pray to move, prayers would move me.

But I am constant as the Northern Star,   65

Of whose true fixed and resting quality

There is no fellow in the firmament.

The skies are painted with unnumbered sparks,

They are all fire, and every one doth shine.

But there's but one in all doth hold his place.   70

So in the world: 'tis furnished well with men,

And men are flesh and blood, and apprehensive.

Yet in the number I do know but one

That unassailable holds on his rank,

Unshaked of motion, and that I am he,   75

Let me a little show it, even in this:

I kick you out of my way like a dog.   50

Know that Caesar does not act unjustly, nor will he act

Without good reason.

METELLUS   Is there no voice here, more worthy than my own,

To sound more sweetly in great Caesar's ear

For the return of my banished brother?   55

BRUTUS   I kiss your hand, but not in flattery, Caesar,

Asking you that Publius Cimber's sentence may

Be immediately repealed.

CAESAR   What, Brutus?

CASSIUS   Pardon, Caesar!   Caesar, pardon!   60

As low as your foot does Cassius fall

To beg for restoring Publius Cimber's citizenship.

CAESAR   I might be persuaded if I were like you.

If I could plead as others do, pleas would move me.

But I am as constant as the North Star,   65

Immovable and stable.

There is no other like it in the heavens.

The skies are painted with innumerable stars,

They are all afire, and every one sparkles.

But only one among them keeps its position.   70

So it is in our world: it's well-supplied with men,

And men are flesh and blood, possessed of reason.

Yet of them all I know of only one

That holds his position without fear of attack,

Undisturbed by outside influence, and I am that one.   75

Let me demonstrate, even on this issue:

That I was constant Cimber should be banished,

And constant do remain to keep him so.

CINNA   O Caesar—

CAESAR   Hence. Wilt thou lift up Olympus?   80

DECIUS   Great Caesar—

CAESAR   Doth not Brutus bootless kneel?

CASCA   Speak, hands, for me! [*He stabs Caesar, the others do also*]

CAESAR   *Et tu, Brute?* Then fall, Caesar. [*He dies*]

CINNA   Liberty! Freedom! Tyranny is dead!   85

   Run hence, proclaim, cry it about the streets.

CASSIUS   Some to the common pulpits, and cry out,

   "Liberty, freedom, and enfranchisement!"

BRUTUS   People and senators, be not affrighted,

   Fly not, stand still! Ambition's debt is paid.   90

CASCA   Go to the pulpit, Brutus.

DECIUS   And Cassius, too.

BRUTUS   Where's Publius?

CINNA   Here, quite confounded with this mutiny.

METELLUS   Stand fast together lest some friend of Caesar's   95

   Should chance—

BRUTUS   Talk not of standing. Publius, good cheer,

   There is no harm intended to your person,

   Nor to no Roman else. So tell them, Publius.

CASSIUS   And leave us, Publius, lest that the people,   100

   Rushing on us, should do your age some mischief.

BRUTUS   Do so, and let no man abide this deed

   But we the doers.

                              Exit all but the conspirators

I was firm that Cimber should be banished,

And I am firm now that he remain so.

CINNA   Oh, Caesar—

CAESAR   Away! Would you try to move Olympus?   80

DECIUS   Great Caesar—

CAESAR   Didn't Brutus kneel in vain?

CASCA   Speak, hands, for me! [*He stabs Caesar, the others do also*]

CAESAR   Even you, Brutus? Then fall, Caesar. [*He dies*]

CINNA   Liberty! Freedom! Tyranny is dead!   85

    Run out from here, proclaim it, shout it in the streets.

CASSIUS   Some run to the public platforms and cry out,

    "Liberty, freedom, and democracy!"

BRUTUS   People and senators, don't be afraid.

    Don't run, stay there! Ambition has paid its debt.   90

CASCA   Go to the podium, Brutus.

DECIUS   And Cassius, too.

BRUTUS   Where's Publius?

CINNA   Here, stunned by the uproar.

METELLUS   Stand close together, in case some friend of Caesar's   95

    Should happen—

BRUTUS   There's no need for that. Publius, be calm,

    There is no harm intended to your person,

    Nor to any other Roman. Tell them so, Publius.

CASSIUS   And leave us, Publius, in case people   100

    Crowding in on us, should injure an elderly man.

BRUTUS   Do so, and let no men suffer the consequences

    But we who have done the deed.

                          Exit all but the conspirators

Enter TREBONIUS

CASSIUS Where is Antony?

TREBONIUS Fled to his house amazed.   105

    Men, wives, and children stare, cry out, and run

    As it were doomsday.

BRUTUS Fates, we will know your pleasures.

    That we shall die we know; 'tis but the time,

    And drawing days out, that men stand upon.   110

CASCA Why, he that cuts off twenty years of life

    Cuts off so many years of fearing death.

BRUTUS Grant that, and then death is a benefit.

    So we are Caesar's friends, that have abridged

    His time of fearing death. Stoop, Romans, stoop,   115

    And let us bathe our hands in Caesar's blood

    Up to the elbows and besmear our swords.

    Then walk we forth, even to the marketplace,

    And waving our red weapons o'er our heads,

    Let's all cry, "Peace, freedom, and liberty!"   120

CASSIUS Stoop then and wash. How many ages hence

    Shall this lofty scene be acted over

    In states unborn and accents yet unknown!

BRUTUS How many times shall Caesar bleed in sport,

    That now on Pompey's basis lies along   125

    No worthier than the dust!

CASSIUS So oft as that shall be,

    So often shall the knot of us be called

    The men that gave their country liberty.

DECIUS What, shall we forth?   130

Enter TREBONIUS

CASSIUS Where is Antony?

TREBONIUS Fled to his house, astounded.   105

    Men, women, and children stare, cry out, and run,

    As if it were doomsday.

BRUTUS We want to know what fate has in store.

    That we will die, we know; it's only when

    And how to prolong the days that concern men.   110

CASCA Why, he that cuts off twenty years of life

    Cuts off that many years of fearing death.

BRUTUS Accept that, and death is a benefit.

    So we are Caesar's friends to have shortened

    His time of fearing death. Bow, Romans, bow,   115

    And let us bathe our hands in Caesar's blood,

    Up to the elbows, and smear our swords.

    Then we'll walk out, as far as the marketplace,

    And waving our bloody weapons over our heads,

    Let's all cry, "Peace, freedom, and liberty."   120

CASSIUS Bow then, and wash. In times to come

    Our noble act will be portrayed

    In nations not yet born and in tongues not yet known.

BRUTUS How many times shall Caesar bleed in plays,

    Who now lies stretched out at the base of Pompey's statue,   125

    Less than the dust.

CASSIUS As often as that shall happen,

    So shall our group be called

    The men who gave their country liberty.

DECIUS Well, shall we go out?   130

CASSIUS Ay, every man away.

    Brutus shall lead, and we will grace his heels

    With the most boldest and best hearts of Rome.

Enter a SERVANT

BRUTUS Soft, who comes here? A friend of Antony's.

SERVANT Thus, Brutus, did my master bid me kneel,   135

    Thus did Mark Antony bid me fall down,

    And, being prostrate, thus he bade me say:

    Brutus is noble, wise, valiant, and honest.

    Caesar was mighty, bold, royal, and loving.

    Say I love Brutus, and I honor him;   140

    Say I feared Caesar, honored him, and loved him.

    If Brutus will vouchsafe that Antony

    May safely come to him and be resolved

    How Caesar hath deserved to lie in death,

    Mark Antony shall not love Caesar dead   145

    So well as Brutus living, but will follow

    The fortunes and affairs of noble Brutus

    Through the hazards of this untrod state

    With all true faith. So says my master Antony.

BRUTUS Thy master is a wise and valiant Roman,   150

    I never thought him worse.

    Tell him, so please him come unto this place,

    He shall be satisfied and by my honor

    Depart untouched.

SERVANT I'll fetch him presently.   155

Exit SERVANT

BRUTUS I know that we shall have him well to friend.

CASSIUS Yes, we must all leave.

    Brutus shall lead, and we will follow behind him

    With the bravest and truest men of Rome.

Enter a SERVANT

BRUTUS Wait a moment. Who's here? A friend of Antony's?

SERVANT Like this, Brutus, did my master tell me to kneel;   135

    Like this did Mark Antony tell me to fall down.

    And, being prostrate before you, he told me to say:

    "Brutus is noble, wise, valiant, and honorable;

    Caesar was mighty, bold, royal, and loving.

    Say I love Brutus, and I honor him;   140

    Say I feared Caesar, honored him, and loved him.

    If Brutus will allow for Antony

    To safely come to him and have explained

    Why Caesar deserved to be killed,

    Mark Antony shall not love the dead Caesar   145

    As well as the living Brutus, but will ally

    Himself with the fortunes and affairs of noble Brutus

    Through the hazards of this unknown situation

    With complete loyalty." So says my master Antony.

BRUTUS Your master is a wise and valiant Roman.   150

    I have never thought otherwise.

    Tell him, if he chooses to come here,

    He shall have an explanation and, upon my honor,

    Will leave unharmed.

SERVANT I'll get him immediately.   155

Exit SERVANT

BRUTUS I know that we shall have him as a good friend.

CASSIUS I wish we may. But yet have I a mind
    That fears him much, and my misgiving still
    Falls shrewdly to the purpose.

Enter ANTONY

BRUTUS But here comes Antony. Welcome, Mark Antony!   160
ANTONY O mighty Caesar! Dost thou lie so low?
    Are all thy conquests, glories, triumphs, spoils
    Shrunk to this little measure? Fare thee well!
    I know not, gentlemen, what you intend,
    Who else must be let blood, who else is rank.   165
    If I myself, there is no hour so fit
    As Caesar's death's hour, nor no instrument
    Of half that worth as those your swords made rich
    With the most noble blood of all this world.
    I do beseech ye, if you bear me hard,   170
    Now, whilst your purpled hands do reek and smoke,
    Fulfil your pleasure. Live a thousand years,
    I shall not find myself so apt to die;
    No place will please me so, no mean of death,
    As here by Caesar, and by you cut off,   175
    The choice and master spirits of this age.
BRUTUS O Antony, beg not your death of us.
    Though now we must appear bloody and cruel,
    As by our hands and this our present act
    You see we do, yet see you but our hands   180
    And this the bleeding business they have done.
    Our hearts you see not, they are pitiful;
    And pity to the general wrong of Rome—

CASSIUS I hope we may. But still I have a feeling
　　　That fears him greatly. And my misgivings
　　　Always turn out to be accurate.

　　　　　　　　　Enter ANTONY

BRUTUS But here comes Antony. Welcome, Mark Antony!　　　160
ANTONY Oh, mighty Caesar! Have you fallen so low?
　　　Are all your conquests, glories, triumphs, and spoils
　　　Shrunk to this little space? Farewell.
　　　I know not, gentlemen, what you intend,
　　　What other blood must be let, who else is ripe.　　　165
　　　If it is I, there is no hour so fit
　　　As Caesar's hour of death, nor any instrument
　　　Half so worthy as those swords of yours made rich
　　　With the most noble blood in all this world.
　　　I beg you, if you bear me ill will,　　　170
　　　Now, while your purpled hands reek and smoke,
　　　Carry out your purpose. If I live a thousand years,
　　　I shall not find myself so ready to die;
　　　No place could please me more, no means of death,
　　　As here by Caesar, cut down by you,　　　175
　　　The finest and master spirits of our time.
BRUTUS Oh, Antony, do not beg us for your death.
　　　Though now we must seem bloody and cruel,
　　　By the color of our hands and this act
　　　You've seen us do, yet you see only our hands　　　180
　　　And this bloody business they have done.
　　　Our hearts, you do not see; they are full of pity.
　　　And pity for the general wrong of Rome—

As fire drives out fire, so pity pity—
Hath done this deed on Caesar. For our part,   185
To you our swords have leaden points, Mark Antony.
Our arms in strength of malice, and our hearts
Of brothers' temper, do receive you in
With all kind love, good thoughts, and reverence.
CASSIUS Your voice shall be as strong as any man's   190
In the disposing of new dignities.
BRUTUS Only be patient till we have appeased
The multitude, beside themselves with fear,
And then we will deliver you the cause
Why I, that did love Caesar when I struck him,   195
Have thus proceeded.
ANTONY I doubt not of your wisdom.
Let each man render me his bloody hand.
First, Marcus Brutus, will I shake with you;
Next, Caius Cassius, do I take your hand;   200
Now, Decius Brutus, yours; now yours, Metellus;
Yours, Cinna; and, my valiant Casca, yours;
Though last, not least in love, yours, good Trebonius.
Gentlemen all—alas, what shall I say?
My credit now stands on such slippery ground   205
That one of two bad ways you must conceit me,
Either a coward or a flatterer.
That I did love thee, Caesar, O, 'tis true!
If then thy spirit look upon us now,
Shall it not grieve thee dearer than thy death   210

As fire drives out fire, pity drives out pity—

Has done this to Caesar. As for you,   185

Our swords have blunted points, Mark Antony.

Our arms, which seem strongly hostile, and our hearts,

Softened by brotherly love, welcome you

With kindest love, good thoughts, and due respect.

CASSIUS Your vote will have as equal weight as any of ours   190

In the granting of new honors.

BRUTUS Just be patient till we have soothed

The people, who are beside themselves with fear,

And then we will give you the reasons

Why I, who loved Caesar when I struck him,   195

Have thus acted.

ANTONY I do not doubt your wisdom.

Let each man give me his bloody hand.

First, Marcus Brutus, I will shake with you;

Next, Caius Cassius, I take your hand;   200

Now, Decius Brutus, yours; now yours, Metellus;

Yours, Cinna; and my valiant, Casca, yours;

Though last, not least in love, yours, good Trebonius.

Gentlemen all—alas, what can I say?

My reputation now stands on slippery ground.   205

You may consider me in one of two bad ways,

Either as a coward or a flatterer.

That I loved you, Caesar, oh, that's true!

If your spirit looks upon us now,

Shall it not grieve you more than your death   210

To see thy Antony making his peace,
Shaking the bloody fingers of thy foes—
Most noble—in the presence of thy corse?
Had I as many eyes as thou hast wounds,
Weeping as fast as they stream forth thy blood,   215
It would become me better than to close
In terms of friendship with thine enemies.
Pardon me, Julius! Here wast thou bayed, brave hart,
Here didst thou fall, and here thy hunters stand,
Signed in thy spoil and crimsoned in thy Lethe.   220
O world! Thou wast the forest to this hart,
And this indeed, O world, the heart of thee.
How like a deer strucken by many princes
Dost thou here lie!

CASSIUS   Mark Antony—   225

ANTONY   Pardon me, Caius Cassius.
The enemies of Caesar shall say this;
Then, in a friend, it is cold modesty.

CASSIUS   I blame you not for praising Caesar so,
But what compact mean you to have with us?   230
Will you be pricked in number of our friends,
Or shall we on and not depend on you?

ANTONY   Therefore I took your hands, but was indeed
Swayed from the point by looking down on Caesar.
Friends am I with you all and love you all,   235
Upon this hope, that you shall give me reasons
Why and wherein Caesar was dangerous.

BRUTUS   Or else were this a savage spectacle.

To see your Antony making his peace,

Shaking the bloody fingers of your foes—

How noble—in the presence of your corpse?

Had I as many eyes as you have wounds,

Weeping as fast as they stream forth your blood,   215

It would be more becoming than to reach

To an agreement with your enemies.

Forgive me, Julius! Here you were cornered, like a brave hart.

Here you fell, and here your hunters stand,

Splattered in your blood, reddened in the stream.   220

Oh, world! You were the forest to this hart,

And this man, indeed, was the heart of the world.

How like a deer struck down by many princes

Do you lie here!

CASSIUS Mark Antony—   225

ANTONY Excuse me, Caius Cassius.

This is what the enemies of Caesar will say.

For a friend, it is calm understatement.

CASSIUS I don't blame you for praising Caesar so,

But what agreement do you mean to have with us?   230

Will you be listed as one of our friends,

Or shall we move on and not count on you?

ANTONY That's why I took your hands, but was indeed

Diverted from my point by looking down on Caesar.

I am friends with you all and love you all   235

And only hope that you shall give me reasons

Showing why and how Caesar was dangerous.

BRUTUS If we could not, this would be a savage spectacle.

Our reasons are so full of good regard
That were you, Antony, the son of Caesar,   240
You should be satisfied.

ANTONY That's all I seek,
And am, moreover, suitor that I may
Produce his body to the marketplace,
And in the pulpit, as becomes a friend,   245
Speak in the order of his funeral.

BRUTUS You shall, Mark Antony.

CASSIUS Brutus, a word with you.
[*Aside to* BRUTUS] You know not what you do. Do not consent
That Antony speak in his funeral.   250
Know you how much the people may be moved
By that which he will utter?

BRUTUS [*Aside to* CASSIUS] By your pardon,
I will myself into the pulpit first
And show the reason of our Caesar's death.   255
What Antony shall speak, I will protest
He speaks by leave and by permission,
And that we are contented Caesar shall
Have all true rites and lawful ceremonies.
It shall advantage more than do us wrong.   260

CASSIUS [*Aside to* BRUTUS] I know not what may fall, I like it not.

BRUTUS Mark Antony, here take you Caesar's body.
You shall not in your funeral speech blame us,
But speak all good you can devise of Caesar
And say you do 't by our permission,   265
Else shall you not have any hand at all

Our reasons are so sound

That were you, Antony, the son of Caesar,   240

You would be satisfied.

ANTONY That's all I seek

And that you will allow me to

Place his body in the marketplace,

And on a platform, as becomes a friend,   245

Speak in the ceremony of his funeral.

BRUTUS You shall, Mark Antony.

CASSIUS Brutus, a word with you.

[*Aside to* BRUTUS] You don't know what you're doing. Don't allow

Antony to speak at the funeral.   250

Do you know how much the people may be moved

By what he says?

BRUTUS [*Aside to* CASSIUS] Excuse me,

I will speak first on the platform

And give the reasons for Caesar's death.   255

What Antony shall say, I will point out,

Is said with our leave and permission,

And that we are agreed that Caesar shall

Have all the proper rites and lawful ceremonies.

It shall do us more good than harm.   260

CASSIUS [*Aside to* BRUTUS] I don't know what will happen. I don't like it.

BRUTUS Mark Antony, here, take your Caesar's body.

You shall not blame us in your funeral speech,

But speak all the good you can of Caesar

And say that you do it with our permission.   265

Otherwise, you shall have no hand at all

About his funeral. And you shall speak

In the same pulpit whereto I am going,

After my speech is ended.

ANTONY Be it so,   270

    I do desire no more.

BRUTUS Prepare the body then and follow us.

Exeunt all but ANTONY

ANTONY O, pardon me, thou bleeding piece of earth,

    That I am meek and gentle with these butchers!

    Thou are the ruins of the noblest man   275

    That ever lived in the tide of times.

    Woe to the hand that shed this costly blood!

    Over thy wounds now do I prophesy—

    Which like dumb mouths do ope their ruby lips

    To beg the voice and utterance of my tongue—   280

    A curse shall light upon the limbs of men;

    Domestic fury and fierce civil strife

    Shall cumber all the parts of Italy;

    Blood and destruction shall be so in use

    And dreadful objects so familiar   285

    That mothers shall but smile when they behold

    Their infants quartered with the hands of war,

    All pity choked with custom of fell deeds;

    And Caesar's spirit, ranging for revenge,

    With Ate by his side come hot from hell, .   290

    Shall in these confines with a monarch's voice

    Cry "Havoc!" and let slip the dogs of war,

In his funeral. And you shall speak

From the same platform that I use,

And after my speech has ended.

ANTONY So be it,   270

    I ask no more.

BRUTUS Prepare the body, then, and follow us.

Exit all but ANTONY

ANTONY Oh, forgive me, you bleeding piece of earth,

    That I am meek and gentle with these butchers!

    You are the ruins of the noblest man   275

    That ever lived in the stream of time.

    Woe to the hand that shed this precious blood!

    Over your wounds do I now make this prophecy—

    Which like dumb mouths open their ruby lips

    To beg me to speak for them—   280

    A curse shall fall upon the bodies of men.

    Domestic turmoil and fierce civil war

    Shall burden all parts of Italy.

    Blood and destruction shall be so common,

    And dreadful deeds so familiar   285

    That mothers shall only smile when they behold

    Their infants cut to pieces by the hands of war,

    All pity choked by familiarity with cruel deeds;

    And Caesar's spirit, scouring the earth for revenge,

    With Ate by his side come hot from hell,   290

    Shall in these regions with a king's voice

    Cry "Havoc!" and unleash the dogs of war,

That this foul deed shall smell above the earth
With carrion men groaning for burial.

Enter Octavius' SERVANT

You serve Octavius Caesar, do you not?   295
SERVANT I do, Mark Antony.
ANTONY Caesar did write for him to come to Rome.
SERVANT He did receive his letters and is coming.
   And bid me say to you by word of mouth—
   O Caesar!   300
ANTONY Thy heart is big, get thee apart and weep.
   Passion, I see, is catching, for mine eyes,
   Seeing those beads of sorrow stand in thine,
   Begin to water. Is thy master coming?
SERVANT He lies tonight within seven leagues of Rome.   305
ANTONY Post back with speed and tell him what hath chanced.
   Here is a mourning Rome, a dangerous Rome,
   No Rome of safety for Octavius yet.
   Hie hence and tell him so. Yet stay awhile,
   Thou shalt not back till I have borne this corse   310
   Into the marketplace. There shall I try
   In my oration how the people take
   The cruel issue of these bloody men,
   According to the which thou shalt discourse
   To young Octavius of the state of things.   315
   Lend me your hand.

                                        Exeunt with Caesar's body

Making this foul deed smell about the earth

Like rotting corpses groaning for burial.

Enter Octavius' SERVANT

You serve Octavius Caesar, do you not?   295

SERVANT   I do, Mark Antony.

ANTONY   Caesar wrote for him to come to Rome.

SERVANT   He received his letters and is coming,

And he told me to say to you personally—

Oh, Caesar   300

ANTONY   Your heart swells with grief; stand aside and weep.

Grief, I see, is catching, for my eyes,

Seeing those tears of sorrow in yours,

Begin to water. Is your master coming?

SERVANT   He is within twenty miles of Rome tonight.   305

ANTONY   Ride back fast and tell him what has happened.

Here is a mourning Rome, a dangerous Rome,

Not a Rome safe for Octavius yet.

Go and tell him so. Yet, wait awhile.

You shall not go back till I have borne this corpse   310

Into the marketplace. There I shall test

In my funeral speech how the people take

The cruel acts of these bloody men,

And you shall then describe

To young Octavius what the situation is.   315

Give me a hand.

They exit with Caesar's body

Scene 2 [*The Marketplace*]

Enter BRUTUS *and* CASSIUS *with the* PLEBEIANS

PLEBEIANS We will be satisfied! Let us be satisfied!

BRUTUS Then follow me and give audience, friends.

Cassius, go you into the other street

And part the numbers.

Those that will hear me speak, let 'em stay here; 5

Those that will follow Cassius, go with him.

And public reasons shall be rendered

Of Caesar's death.

FIRST PLEBEIAN I will hear Brutus speak.

SECOND PLEBEIAN I will hear Cassius and compare their reasons 10

When severally we hear them rendered.

Exit CASSIUS *with some* PLEBEIANS

[BRUTUS *goes to the platform*]

THIRD PLEBEIAN The noble Brutus is ascended, silence!

BRUTUS Be patient till the last.

Romans, countrymen, and lovers, hear me for my cause, and be silent

that you may hear. Believe me for mine honor, and have respect to 15

mine honor that you may believe. Censure me in your wisdom, and

awake your senses that you may the better judge. If there be any in this

assembly, any dear friend of Caesar's, to him I say that Brutus' love to

Caesar was no less than his. If then that friend demand why Brutus

rose against Caesar, this is my answer: not that I loved Caesar less, 20

but that I loved Rome more. Had you rather Caesar were living, and

die all slaves, than that Caesar were dead, to live all freemen? As

Caesar loved me, I weep for him; as he was fortunate, I rejoice at it;

Scene 2 [*The Marketplace*]

        Enter BRUTUS *and* CASSIUS *with* CITIZENS

CITIZENS We will have an explanation! Give us answers!

BRUTUS Then follow me and listen, friends.

    Cassius, go into the other street

    And divide the crowd.

    Those who want to hear me speak, let them stay here;   5

    Those who want Cassius, go with him.

    And reasons concerning the public good shall be given

    For Caesar's death.

FIRST CITIZEN I will hear Brutus speak.

SECOND CITIZEN I will hear Cassius. We'll hear their reasons   10

    separately and then compare them.

              Exit CASSIUS *with some* CITIZENS

[BRUTUS *goes to the platform*]

THIRD CITIZEN The noble Brutus is on the platform. Silence!

BRUTUS Be patient till the end of my speech.

  Romans, countrymen, and dear friends, hear me for the cause I represent,

  and be silent that you may hear. Believe me for my honor, and respect 15

  my honor so that you may believe. Judge me in your wisdom. Let your

  reason be alert so that you may better judge. If there be any in this

  assembly, any dear friend of Caesar's, to him I say that Brutus' love for

  Caesar was no less than his. If, then, that friend asks why Brutus rose

  against Caesar, this is my answer: Not that I loved Caesar less, but that 20

  I loved Rome more. Would you rather Caesar were alive, and all die

  slaves, or that Caesar were dead, and all live freemen? Because

  Caesar loved me, I weep for him; as he was fortunate, I rejoiced;

As he was valiant, I honor him; but, as he was ambitious, I
slew him. There is tears for his love, joy for his fortune, honor 25
for his valor, and death for his ambition. Who is here so base
that would be a bondman? If any, speak, for him have I offended.
Who is here so rude that would not be a Roman? If any, speak,
for him I have offended. Who is here so vile that will not love his
country? If any, speak, for him have I offended. I pause for 30
a reply.

PLEBEIANS None, Brutus, none.

BRUTUS Then none have I offended. I have done no more to Caesar
than you shall do to Brutus. The question of his death is enrolled
in the Capitol, his glory not extenuated wherein he was worthy, nor 35
his offenses enforced for which he suffered death.

       Enter MARK ANTONY *and others with Caesar's body*

Here comes his body, mourned by Mark Antony, who, though
he had no hand in his death, shall receive the benefit of his
dying, a place in the commonwealth, as which of you shall not?
With this I depart: that, as I slew my best lover for the good 40
of Rome, I have the same dagger of myself when it shall please
my country to need my death.

[*He descends*]

PLEBEIANS Live, Brutus, live, live!

FIRST PLEBEIAN Bring him with triumph home unto his house.

SECOND PLEBEIAN Give him a statue with his ancestors. 45

THIRD PLEBEIAN Let him be Caesar.

FOURTH PLEBEIAN Caesar's better parts
    Shall be crowned in Brutus.

As he was valiant, I honor him; but, as he was ambitious, I
killed him. There are tears for his love; joy for his fortune; honor   25
for his valor; and death for his ambition. Who is here so lowly that
he would be a slave? If there is one, speak, for I have harmed him.
Who is here so barbarous that he would not be a Roman? If there is
one, speak, for I have harmed him. Who is here so vile that he does
not love his country? If there is one, speak, for I have harmed him.   30
I pause for a reply.

CITIZENS None, Brutus, none.

BRUTUS Then I have harmed no one. I have done no more to Caesar
than you may do to Brutus. The circumstances of his death are on
record in the Capitol, his glory, which did him honor, not belittled,   35
nor his offenses, for which he died, over-stressed.

      Enter MARK ANTONY *and others with Caesar's body*
Here comes his body, mourned by Mark Antony who, though
he had no hand in Caesar's death, shall benefit from his dying,
taking his rightful place in the republic, as shall you all. With
this, I'll leave you: Just as I killed my best friend for the good   40
of Rome, I will use that same dagger on myself when my country
decides it needs my death.

[*He descends*]

CITIZENS Live, Brutus, live, live!

FIRST CITIZEN Take him in triumph to his house.

SECOND CITIZEN Give him a statue among his ancestors.   45

THIRD CITIZEN Let him be Caesar!

FOURTH CITIZEN Only Caesar's good qualities
    Shall be crowned in Brutus.

FIRST PLEBEIAN We'll bring him to his house

    With shouts and clamors.   50

BRUTUS My countrymen—

SECOND PLEBEIAN Peace, silence, Brutus speaks!

FIRST PLEBEIAN Peace ho!

BRUTUS Good countrymen, let me depart alone,

    And, for my sake, stay here with Antony.   55

    Do grace to Caesar's corpse, and grace his speech

    Tending to Caesar's glories, which Mark Antony

    (By our permission) is allowed to make.

    I do entreat you, not a man depart,

    Save I alone, till Antony have spoke.   60

He exits

FIRST PLEBEIAN Stay ho, and let us hear Mark Antony.

THIRD PLEBEIAN Let him go up into the public chair,

    We'll hear him. Noble Antony, go up.

ANTONY For Brutus' sake, I am beholding to you.

[*He goes to the platform*]

FOURTH PLEBEIAN What does he say of Brutus?   65

THIRD PLEBEIAN He says for Brutus' sake

    He finds himself beholding to us all.

FOURTH PLEBEIAN 'Twere best he speak no harm of Brutus here!

FIRST PLEBEIAN This Caesar was a tyrant.

THIRD PLEBEIAN Nay, that's certain.   70

    We are blest that Rome is rid of him.

SECOND PLEBEIAN Peace, let us hear what Antony can say.

ANTONY You gentle Romans—

PLEBEIANS Peace ho, let us hear him.

FIRST CITIZEN We'll take him to his house
    With shouts and cheers. 50
BRUTUS My countrymen—
SECOND CITIZEN Peace, silence, Brutus speaks!
FIRST CITIZEN Quiet there!
BRUTUS Good countrymen, let me depart alone,
    And, for my sake, stay here with Antony. 55
    Honor Caesar's corpse and listen to Antony's speech
    About the glories of Caesar, which he
    (By our permission) is allowed to make.
    I beg you, let no man leave,
    Except for myself, till Antony has spoken. 60

He exits

FIRST CITIZEN Stay here, and let us hear Mark Antony.
THIRD CITIZEN Let him go up onto the platform.
    We'll hear him. Noble Antony, go up.
ANTONY On behalf of Brutus, I am indebted to you.
[*He goes to the platform*]
FOURTH CITIZEN What does he say of Brutus? 65
THIRD CITIZEN He says on behalf of Brutus
    He is indebted to us all.
FOURTH CITIZEN He better not say anything against Brutus here!
FIRST CITIZEN This Caesar was a tyrant.
THIRD CITIZEN Yes, that's for certain. 70
    We are blessed that Rome is rid of him.
SECOND CITIZEN Quiet, let us hear what Antony has to say.
ANTONY You gentle Romans—
CITIZENS Quiet, let us hear him.

ANTONY Friends, Romans, countrymen, lend me your ears!   75
    I come to bury Caesar, not to praise him.
    The evil that men do lives after them,
    The good is oft interred with their bones.
    So let it be with Caesar. The noble Brutus
    Hath told you Caesar was ambitious;   80
    If it were so, it was a grievous fault,
    And grievously hath Caesar answered it
    Here, under leave of Brutus and the rest—
    For Brutus is an honorable man,
    So are they all, all honorable men—   85
    Come I to speak in Caesar's funeral.
    He was my friend, faithful and just to me,
    But Brutus says he was ambitious,
    And Brutus is an honorable man.
    He hath brought many captives home to Rome,   90
    Whose ransoms did the general coffers fill.
    Did this in Caesar seem ambitious?
    When that the poor have cried, Caesar hath wept.
    Ambition should be made of sterner stuff;
    Yet Brutus says he was ambitious,   95
    And Brutus is an honorable man.
    You did see that on the Lupercal
    I thrice presented him a kingly crown,
    Which he did thrice refuse. Was this ambition?
    Yet Brutus says he was ambitious,   100
    And sure he is an honorable man.

ANTONY Friends, Romans, countrymen, lend me your ears! 75
   I've come to bury Caesar, not to praise him.
   The evil that men do lives after them,
   The good is often buried with their bones.
   So let it be with Caesar. The noble Brutus
   Has told you Caesar was ambitious; 80
   If that is true, it is a grievous fault,
   And grievously has Caesar paid for it.
   Here, by leave of Brutus and the others—
   For Brutus is an honorable man,
   So are they all, all honorable men— 85
   I come to speak at Caesar's funeral.
   He was my friend, faithful and just to me,
   But Brutus says he was ambitious,
   And Brutus is an honorable man.
   Caesar brought many captives home to Rome, 90
   Whose ransoms filled the public treasury.
   Did this seem ambitious in Caesar?
   When the poor have cried, Caesar has wept.
   Ambition should be made of sterner stuff;
   Yet Brutus says he was ambitious, 95
   And Brutus is an honorable man.
   You saw on the feast of Lupercal
   I thrice presented him with a kingly crown;
   Three times he refused. Was this ambition?
   Yet Brutus says he was ambitious, 100
   And surely he is an honorable man.

I speak not to disprove what Brutus spoke,
But here I am to speak what I do know.
You all did love him once, not without cause;
What cause withholds you then to mourn for him? 105
O judgment, thou are fled to brutish beasts,
And men have lost their reason! Bear with me,
My heart is in the coffin there with Caesar,
And I must pause till it come back to me.

FIRST PLEBEIAN Methinks there is much reason in his sayings. 110

SECOND PLEBEIAN If thou consider rightly of the matter,
Caesar has had great wrong.

THIRD PLEBEIAN Has he, masters?
I fear there will a worse come in his place.

FOURTH PLEBEIAN Marked ye his words? He would not take 115
the crown.
Therefore 'tis certain he was not ambitious.

FIRST PLEBEIAN If it be found so, some will dear abide it.

SECOND PLEBEIAN Poor soul, his eyes are red as fire with weeping.

THIRD PLEBEIAN There's not a nobler man in Rome than Antony. 120

FOURTH PLEBEIAN Now mark him, he begins again to speak.

ANTONY But yesterday the word of Caesar might
Have stood against the world; now lies he there,
And none so poor to do him reverence.
O masters, if I were disposed to stir 125
Your hearts and minds to mutiny and rage,
I should do Brutus wrong and Cassius wrong,
Who (you all know) are honorable men.
I will not do them wrong. I rather choose

I don't speak to dispute what Brutus said,

But I am here to tell just what I know.

You all loved Caesar once, and not without reason;

What reason then prevents you from mourning now?   105

Oh, wisdom, even beasts know how to mourn,

Only men have lost their reason! Bear with me.

My heart is in the coffin there with Caesar,

And I must pause till it comes back to me.

FIRST CITIZEN I think there's a lot of sense in what he says.   110

SECOND CITIZEN If you think about it properly,

Caesar has been greatly wronged.

THIRD CITIZEN Has he, friends?

I fear someone worse will take his place.

FOURTH CITIZEN Did you note his words, "He would not take   115

the crown."

It's certain, therefore, he was not ambitious.

FIRST CITIZEN If that is true, someone will pay dearly for it.

SECOND CITIZEN Poor soul, his eyes are red as fire from weeping.

THIRD CITIZEN There's not a nobler man in Rome than Antony.   120

FOURTH CITIZEN Now listen, he starts to speak again.

ANTONY Only yesterday the word of Caesar would

Have stood against the world; now he lies there,

And no man so poor as to pay him respect.

Oh, friends, if I were inclined to stir   125

Your hearts and minds to mutiny and riot,

I should wrong Brutus and wrong Cassius

Who (you all know) are honorable men.

I will not do them wrong. Instead, I choose

To wrong the dead, to wrong myself and you, 130

Than I will wrong such honorable men.

But here's a parchment with the seal of Caesar.

I found it in his closet. 'Tis his will.

Let but the commons hear this testament—

Which, pardon me, I do not mean to read— 135

And they would go and kiss dead Caesar's wounds

And dip their napkins in his sacred blood,

Yea, beg a hair of him for memory,

And, dying, mention it within their wills,

Bequeathing it as a rich legacy 140

Unto their issue.

FOURTH PLEBEIAN We'll hear the will. Read it, Mark Antony.

PLEBEIANS The will, the will, we will hear Caesar's will!

ANTONY Have patience, gentle friends, I must not read it.

It is not meet you know how Caesar loved you. 145

You are not wood, you are not stones, but men,

And being men, hearing the will of Caesar,

It will inflame you, it will make you mad.

'Tis good you know not that you are his heirs,

For if you should, O, what would come of it? 150

FOURTH PLEBEIAN Read the will, we'll hear it, Antony.

You shall read us the will, Caesar's will!

ANTONY Will you be patient? Will you stay awhile?

I have o'ershot myself to tell you of it.

I fear I wrong the honorable men 155

Whose daggers have stabbed Caesar, I do fear it.

FOURTH PLEBEIAN They were traitors. Honorable men?

To wrong the dead, to wrong myself and you, 130
Than to wrong such honorable men.
But here's a document with the seal of Caesar.
I found it in his study. It's his will.
If the common people were to hear this testament—
Which, pardon me, I do not mean to read— 135
They would go and kiss dead Caesar's wounds
And dip cloths in his precious blood,
Yes, beg one of his hairs as a souvenir,
And, after death, mention it in their wills,
Bequeathing it as a rich legacy 140
To their children.

FOURTH CITIZEN We want to hear the will. Read it, Mark Antony.

CITIZENS The will, the will, we will hear Caesar's will.

ANTONY Have patience, gentle friends, I must not read it.
It is not fitting for you to know how Caesar loved you. 145
You're not made of wood, you are not stones, but men,
And being men, hearing Caesar's will,
It will inflame you, it will make you mad.
It's good you don't know you are his heirs,
For if you should, Oh, what would happen then? 150

FOURTH CITIZEN Read the will. We'll hear it, Antony.
You shall read us the will, Caesar's will!

ANTONY Will you be patient? Will you wait awhile?
I have gone farther than I should to tell you of it.
I fear I wrong the honorable men 155
Whose daggers have stabbed Caesar. I really fear it.

FOURTH CITIZEN They were traitors. Honorable men?

PLEBEIANS The will! The testament!

SECOND PLEBEIAN They were villains, murders! The will, read the will!

ANTONY You will compel me then to read the will?   160

    Then make a ring about the corpse of Caesar,

    And let me show you him that made the will.

    Shall I descend? And will you give me leave?

PLEBEIANS Come down.

SECOND PLEBEIAN Descend.   165

THIRD PLEBEIAN You shall have leave.

[ANTONY *descends*]

FOURTH PLEBEIAN A ring, stand round.

FIRST PLEBEIAN Stand from the hearse. Stand from the body.

SECOND PLEBEIAN Room for Antony, most noble Antony.

ANTONY Nay, press not so upon me. Stand far off.   170

PLEBEIANS Stand back! Room, bear back!

ANTONY If you have tears, prepare to shed them now.

    You all do know this mantle. I remember

    The first time ever Caesar put it on,

    'Twas on a summer's evening, in his tent,   175

    That day he overcame the Nervii.

    Look, in this place ran Cassius' dagger through.

    See what a rent the envious Casca made.

    Through this the well-beloved Brutus stabbed,

    And as he plucked his cursed steel away,   180

    Mark how the blood of Caesar followed it,

    As rushing out of doors to be resolved

    If Brutus so unkindly knocked or no,

    For Brutus, as you know, was Caesar's angel.

CITIZENS The will! The testament!

SECOND CITIZEN They were villains, murderers! The will, read the will!

ANTONY You will compel me to read the will, then?   160

    Then make a ring around the corpse of Caesar,

    And let me show you the man who made the will.

    Shall I descend? Do I have your permission?

CITIZENS Come down.

SECOND CITIZEN Descend.   165

THIRD CITIZEN You have our permission.

[ANTONY *descends*]

FOURTH CITIZEN Form a ring, stand around.

FIRST CITIZEN Stand away from the bier, away from the body.

SECOND CITIZEN Make room for Antony, most noble Antony,

ANTONY No, don't crowd me. Stand farther off.   170

CITIZENS Stand back! Room, move back!

ANTONY If you have tears, prepare to shed them now.

    You all know this cloak. I remember

    The first time that Caesar put it on.

    It was a summer evening in his tent,   175

    The day he defeated the Nervii.

    Look, this is where Cassius' dagger went through.

    See what a tear the malicious Casca made.

    Through this, the well-loved Brutus stabbed,

    And as he pulled his cursed steel out,   180

    Note how the blood of Caesar followed it,

    As though rushing out of doors to see

    Whether or not Brutus had so unkindly knocked.

    For Brutus, as you know, was Caesar's angel.

Judge, O you gods, how dearly Caesar loved him!   185
This was the most unkindest cut of all.
For when the noble Caesar saw him stab,
Ingratitude, more strong than traitor's arms,
Quite vanquished him. Then burst his mighty heart,
And, in his mantle muffling up his face,   190
Even at the base of Pompey's statue
(Which all the while ran blood) great Caesar fell.
O, what a fall was there, my countrymen!
Then I, and you, and all of us fell down,
Whilst bloody treason flourished over us.   195
O, now you weep, and I perceive you feel
The dint of pity. These are gracious drops.
Kind souls, what, weep you when you but behold
Our Caesar's vesture wounded? Look you here,
Here is himself, marred as you see with traitors.   200
FIRST PLEBEIAN O piteous spectacle!
SECOND PLEBEIAN O noble Caesar!
THIRD PLEBEIAN O woeful day!
FOURTH PLEBEIAN O traitors, villains!
FIRST PLEBEIAN O most bloody sight!   205
SECOND PLEBEIAN We will be revenged!
PLEBEIANS Revenge! About! Seek! Burn! Fire! Kill!
     Slay! Let not a traitor live!
ANTONY Stay, countrymen.
FIRST PLEBEIAN Peace there, hear the noble Antony.   210
SECOND PLEBEIAN We'll hear him, we'll follow him,
     we'll die with him.

Judge, oh you gods, how dearly Caesar loved him!   185
His was the cruelest cut of all.
When the noble Caesar saw him stab,
Ingratitude, stronger than the traitor's arms,
Quite overcame him. Then his mighty heart burst.
And with his cloak covering up his face,   190
Here at the base of Pompey's statue
(Which all the while ran with blood) great Caesar fell.
Oh, what a fall it was, my countrymen!
Then I, and you, and all of us fell down,
While bloody treason flourished their weapons.   195
Oh, now you weep, and I perceive you feel
The force of pity. These are gracious tears.
Kind souls, what, do you weep at the sight of
Caesar's wounded garment? Then look here.
Here he is himself, mutilated, as you see, by traitors.   200
FIRST CITIZEN   Oh, pitiful sight!
SECOND CITIZEN   Oh, noble Caesar!
THIRD CITIZEN   Oh, sad day!
FOURTH CITIZEN   Oh, traitors, villains!
FIRST CITIZEN   Oh, most bloody sight!   205
SECOND CITIZEN   We will be avenged!
CITIZENS   Revenge! Come on! Seek the traitors! Burn! Fire! Kill!
    Slay! Let not a single traitor live!
ANTONY   Wait, countrymen.
FIRST CITIZEN   Quiet there, hear the noble Antony.   210
SECOND CITIZEN   We'll hear him, we'll follow him,
    we'll die with him.

ANTONY Good friends, sweet friends, let me not stir you up

To such a sudden flood of mutiny.

They that have done this deed are honorable.   215

What private griefs they have, alas, I know not,

That made them do it. They are wise and honorable,

And will no doubt with reasons answer you.

I come not, friends, to steal away your hearts.

I am no orator, as Brutus is,   220

But—as you know me all—a plain blunt man

That love my friend, and that they know full well

That gave me public leave to speak of him.

For I have neither wit, nor words, nor worth,

Action, nor utterance, nor the power of speech   225

To stir men's blood. I only speak right on.

I tell you that which you yourselves do know,

Show you sweet Caesar's wounds, poor, poor

　　　　dumb mouths,

And bid them speak for me. But were I Brutus,   230

And Brutus Antony, there were an Antony

Would ruffle up your spirits and put a tongue

In every wound of Caesar, that should move

The stones of Rome to rise and mutiny.

PLEBEIANS We'll mutiny.   235

FIRST PLEBEIAN We'll burn the house of Brutus.

THIRD PLEBEIAN Away, then, come, seek the conspirators.

ANTONY Yet hear me, countrymen, yet hear me speak.

PLEBEIANS Peace ho, hear Antony, most noble Antony!

ANTONY Why, friends, you go to do you know not what.   240

ANTONY Good friends, sweet friends, don't let me stir you up

    To such a surge of violence.

    They who have done this deed are honorable. 215

    What personal grudges they had, alas, I do not know,

    That made them do it. They are wise and honorable

    And will no doubt provide you with answers.

    I do not come, friends, to steal away your hearts.

    I am no orator, as Brutus is, 220

    But—as you all know—a plain blunt man

    Who loved his friend, and they know this well

    Who gave me permission to speak in public of him.

    I have neither the intellect nor the words nor the power,

    The gestures nor the delivery nor the eloquence 225

    To stir men's blood. I only speak right on.

    I tell you what you yourselves already know,

    Show you sweet Caesar's wounds, poor, poor

        dumb mouths,

    And ask them to speak for me. But if I were Brutus 230

    And Brutus Antony, then there would be an Antony

    To arouse your emotions and put a tongue

    To every wound of Caesar that would move

    The stones of Rome to rise and riot.

CITIZENS We'll riot. 235

FIRST CITIZEN We'll burn the house of Brutus.

THIRD CITIZEN Let's go, then. Come on. Find the conspirators.

ANTONY Listen to me, countrymen, hear me speak.

CITIZENS Quiet. Listen to Antony, most noble Antony!

ANTONY Why, friends, you don't know what you're doing. 240

131

Wherein hath Caesar thus deserved your loves?

Alas, you know not! I must tell you then.

You have forgot the will I told you of.

PLEBEIANS Most true. The will, let's stay and hear the will.

ANTONY Here is the will, and under Caesar's seal.   245

    To every Roman citizen he gives,

    To every several man, seventy-five drachmas.

SECOND PLEBEIAN Most noble Caesar, we'll revenge his death!

THIRD PLEBEIAN O royal Caesar!

ANTONY Hear me with patience.   250

PLEBEIANS Peace ho!

ANTONY Moreover, he hath left you all his walks,

    His private arbors, and new-planted orchards,

    On this side Tiber; he hath left them you,

    And to your heirs forever—common pleasures,   255

    To walk abroad and recreate yourselves.

    Here was a Caesar! When comes such another?

FIRST PLEBEIAN Never, never! Come, away, away!

    We'll burn his body in the holy place

    And with the brands fire the traitors' houses.   260

    Take up the body.

SECOND PLEBEIAN Go fetch fire!

THIRD PLEBEIAN Pluck down benches!

FOURTH PLEBEIAN Pluck down forms, windows, anything!

Exeunt Plebeians with the body

ANTONY Now let it work, Mischief, thou art afoot,   265

    Take thou what course thou wilt!

What has Caesar done to deserve your love?

Alas, you don't know! Then I must tell you.

You have forgotten the will I told you about.

CITIZENS That's true. The will, let's stay and hear the will.

ANTONY Here is the will, with Caesar's own seal.   245

To every Roman citizen he gives,

To each individual man, seventy-five drachmas.

SECOND CITIZEN Most noble Caesar, we'll revenge his death!

THIRD CITIZEN O generous Caesar!

ANTONY Hear me with patience.   250

CITIZENS Quiet now!

ANTONY Moreover, he has left you all his walks,

His private arbors, and newly planted orchards

On this side of the Tiber. He has left them to you

And to your heirs, forever—public parks   255

To walk in and to enjoy yourselves.

Here was a Caesar. When will we see his kind again?

FIRST CITIZEN Never, never! Come on, come on!

We'll burn his body in the holy place

And use the brands to fire the traitors' houses.   260

Take up the body.

SECOND CITIZEN Go and get fire.

THIRD CITIZEN Pull down benches.

FOURTH CITIZEN Pull down long benches, shutters, anything!

Exit CITIZENS *with the body*

ANTONY Now, let it work itself out. Destruction, you have begun.   265

Take whatever course you will!

Enter SERVANT

How now, fellow?

SERVANT Sir, Octavius is already come to Rome.

ANTONY Where is he?

SERVANT He and Lepidus are at Caesar's house.

ANTONY And thither will I straight to visit him.   270

He comes upon a wish. Fortune is merry,

And in this mood will give us anything.

SERVANT I heard him say Brutus and Cassius

Are rid like madmen through the gates of Rome.

ANTONY Belike they had some notice of the people,   275

How I moved them. Bring me to Octavius.

Exeunt

Scene 3 [*A street in Rome*]

Enter CINNA *the poet and after him the* PLEBEIANS

CINNA I dreamt tonight that I did feast with Caesar,

And things unluckily charge my fantasy.

I have no will to wander forth of doors,

Yet something leads me forth.

FIRST PLEBEIAN What is your name?   5

SECOND PLEBEIAN Whither are you going?

THIRD PLEBEIAN Where do you dwell?

FOURTH PLEBEIAN Are you a married man or a bachelor?

SECOND PLEBEIAN Answer every man directly.

FIRST PLEBEIAN Ay, and briefly.   10

FOURTH PLEBEIAN Ay, and wisely.

THIRD PLEBEIAN Ay, and truly, you were best.

Enter SERVANT

Yes, you want me?

SERVANT   Sir, Octavius has already arrived in Rome.

ANTONY   Where is he?

SERVANT   He and Lepidus are at Caesar's house.

ANTONY   And I will go straight there to visit him.   270

He comes just when I want. Fortune smiles,

And in this mood will give us anything.

SERVANT   I heard him say Brutus and Cassius

Have ridden like madmen through the gates of Rome.

ANTONY   Probably they have had reports of how   275

I moved the people. Take me to Octavius.

They exit

Scene 3   [*A street in Rome*]

Enter CINNA *the poet and after him the* CITIZENS

CINNA   I dreamed last night I dined with Caesar,

And things of ill omen burden my imagination.

I don't wish to go outside,

But something leads me forth.

FIRST CITIZEN   What is your name?   5

SECOND CITIZEN   Where are you going?

THIRD CITIZEN   Where do you live?

FOURTH CITIZEN   Are you a married man or a bachelor?

SECOND CITIZEN   Answer each man fully.

FIRST CITIZEN   Yes, and briefly.   10

FOURTH CITIZEN   Yes, and wisely.

THIRD CITIZEN   Yes, and the truth, if you know what's best.

CINNA What is my name? Whither am I going? Where do I dwell?
    Am I a married man or a bachelor? Then to answer every
    man directly and briefly, wisely and truly. Wisely I say I   15
    am a bachelor.

SECOND PLEBEIAN That's as much as to say they are fools that marry.
    You'll bear me a bang for that, I fear. Proceed directly.

CINNA Directly I am going to Caesar's funeral.

FIRST PLEBEIAN As a friend or an enemy?   20

CINNA As a friend.

SECOND PLEBEIAN That matter is answered directly.

FOURTH PLEBEIAN For your dwelling—briefly.

CINNA Briefly, I dwell by the Capitol.

THIRD PLEBEIAN Your name, sir, truly.   25

CINNA Truly, my name is Cinna.

FIRST PLEBEIAN Tear him to pieces, he's a conspirator.

CINNA I am Cinna the poet, I am Cinna the poet.

FOURTH PLEBEIAN Tear him for his bad verses, tear him
    for his bad verses.   30

CINNA I am not Cinna the conspirator.

FOURTH PLEBEIAN It is no matter, his name's Cinna. Pluck but
    his name out of his heart and turn him going.

THIRD PLEBEIAN Tear him, tear him! Come, brands ho, firebrands! To
    Brutus', to Cassius', burn all! Some to Decius' house, and some   35
    to Casca's, some to Ligarius'! Away, go!

                        Exeunt PLEBEIANS, *dragging* CINNA

CINNA What is my name? Where am I going? Where do I live? Am
    I a married man or a bachelor? Then I am to answer every man
    fully and briefly, wisely and truly. Wisely, I say I   15
    am a bachelor.

SECOND CITIZEN That's as much as to say they are fools that marry.
    You'll get a blow from me for that. Proceed directly.

CINNA Directly, I am going to Caesar's funeral.

FIRST CITIZEN As a friend or as an enemy?   20

CINNA As a friend.

SECOND CITIZEN That's a direct answer.

FOURTH CITIZEN Where do you live—briefly.

CINNA Briefly, I live near the Capitol.

THIRD CITIZEN Your name, sir, truly.   25

CINNA Truly, my name is Cinna.

FIRST CITIZEN Tear him to pieces, he's a conspirator.

CINNA I am Cinna the poet, I am Cinna the poet.

FOURTH CITIZEN Tear him to pieces for his bad verses, tear him to
    pieces for his bad verses.   30

CINNA I am not Cinna the conspirator.

FOURTH CITIZEN It doesn't matter, his name's Cinna. Tear his name
    out of him and send him packing.

THIRD CITIZEN Tear him, tear him! Come on, some wood, some torches!
    To Brutus' house, to Cassius', burn them all! Some go to Decius'   35
    house, and some to Casca's, some to Ligarius'! Away with you, go!

                                            Exit CITIZENS, *dragging* CINNA

Act Four

Scene 1 [*A room in* Antony's *house*]

Enter ANTONY, OCTAVIUS, *and* LEPIDUS

ANTONY These men then shall die, their names are pricked.

OCTAVIUS Your brother too must die; consent you, Lepidus?

LEPIDUS I do consent—

OCTAVIUS Prick him down, Antony.

LEPIDUS Upon condition Publius shall not live,   5

    Who is your sister's son, Mark Antony.

ANTONY He shall not live; look, with a spot I damn him.

    But, Lepidus, go you to Caesar's house,

    Fetch the will hither, and we shall determine

    How to cut off some charge in legacies.   10

LEPIDUS What, shall I find you here?

OCTAVIUS Or here or at the Capitol.

                               Exit LEPIDUS

ANTONY This is a slight, unmeritable man,

    Meet to be sent on errands; is it fit,

    The threefold world divided, he should stand   15

    One of the three to share it?

OCTAVIUS   So you thought him

    And took his voice who should be pricked to die

    In our black sentence and proscription.

ANTONY Octavius, I have seen more days than you,   20

    And though we lay these honors on this man

    To ease ourselves of divers slanderous loads,

    He shall but bear them as the ass bears gold,

138

Act Four

Scene 1 [*A room in* Antony's *house*]

Enter ANTONY, OCTAVIUS, *and* LEPIDUS

ANTONY These men, then, shall die. Their names are marked.

OCTAVIUS Your brother, too, must die. Do you agree, Lepidus?

LEPIDUS I do agree—

OCTAVIUS Mark him down, Antony.

LEPIDUS Upon condition Publius shall also die,   5

    The one who is your sister's son, Mark Antony.

ANTONY Look. He shall not live. With a mark I condemn him.

    Lepidus, go now to Caesar's house,

    Bring the will here, and we shall determine

    How to reduce the expense of the legacies.   10

LEPIDUS Will you still be here?

OCTAVIUS Either here or at the Capitol.

Exit LEPIDUS

ANTONY This is a slight, insignificant man,

    Good for sending on errands; is it fitting,

    With our world divided in three, that he should be   15

    One of the three to have a share?

OCTAVIUS So you thought once

    And asked his opinion who should be marked to die

    On our black list of death and exile.

ANTONY Octavius, I am older than you,   20

    And though we lay these honors on this man

    To bear the brunt of unpopular decisions,

    He carries this burden as an ass bears gold,

To groan and sweat under the business,

Either led or driven, as we point the way; 25

And having brought our treasure where we will,

Then take we down his load and turn him off

(Like to the empty ass) to shake his ears

And graze in commons.

OCTAVIUS You may do your will 30

But he's a tried and valiant soldier.

ANTONY So is my horse, Octavius, and for that

I do appoint his store of provender.

It is a creature that I teach to fight,

To wind, to stop, to run directly on, 35

His corporal motion governed by my spirit.

And, in some taste, is Lepidus but so.

He must be taught and trained and bid go forth,

A barren-spirited fellow, one that feeds

On objects, arts, and imitations, 40

Which, out of use and staled by other men,

Begin his fashion. Do not talk of him

But as a property. And now, Octavius,

Listen great things. Brutus and Cassius

Are levying powers; we must straight make head. 45

Therefore let our alliance be combined,

Our best friends made, our means stretched,

And let us presently go sit in counsel,

How covert matters may be best disclosed

And open perils surest answered. 50

Groaning and sweating under the hard labor,

Being led or driven, according to the way we point;   25

And having brought our treasure where we wish,

Then we remove the load and turn him loose

(Like the ass set free) to shake his ears

And graze on the public pasture.

OCTAVIUS You may do as you wish,   30

    But he's a tried and valiant soldier.

ANTONY So is my horse, Octavius, and for that

    I give him a supply of food.

    It is a creature that I teach to fight,

    To wheel, to stop, to run directly ahead,   35

    His physical movements controlled by my mind.

    And, to some degree, Lepidus is like that.

    He must be taught and trained and told when to go,

    An uninspired fellow, one who seizes

    On curiosities, artifices, and imitations   40

    That, out of use and made common by other men,

    He thinks the latest fashion. Do not talk of him

    Except as a tool. But now, Octavius,

    Hear some important matters. Brutus and Cassius

    Are raising armies; we must raise a force.   45

    Therefore, let our allied forces be combined,

    Our closest allies selected, and resources employed,

    And let us immediately consider

    How hidden dangers may be revealed

    And obvious perils best answered.   50

OCTAVIUS Let us do so, for we are at the stake

    And bayed about with many enemies,

    And some that smile have in their hearts, I fear,

    Millions of mischiefs.

Exeunt

Scene 2 [*A military camp in Sardis, a city in Asia Minor*]
Drum. Enter LUCILIUS, PINDARUS, *and* SOLDIERS;

            enter BRUTUS *and* LUCIUS *from Brutus' tent*

BRUTUS Stand ho!

LUCILIUS Give the word ho, and stand!

BRUTUS What now, Lucilius, is Cassius near?

LUCILIUS He is at hand, and Pindarus is come

    To do you salutation from his master.   5

BRUTUS He greets me well. Your master, Pindarus,

    In his own change or by ill officers,

    Hath given me some worthy cause to wish

    Things done undone, but if he be at hand

    I shall be satisfied.   10

PINDARUS I do not doubt

    But that my noble master will appear

    Such as he is, full of regard and honor.

BRUTUS He is not doubted.

    [*Aside to* LUCILIUS] A word, Lucilius,   15

    How he received you; let me be resolved.

LUCILIUS With courtesy and respect enough,

    But not with such familiar instances,

    Nor with such free and friendly conference,

OCTAVIUS Let us do so, for we are chained to a stake
    And hounded with many enemies,
    And some who smile have in their hearts, I fear,
    Millions of dangerous thoughts.

They exit

Scene 2 [*A military camp in Sardis, a city in Asia Minor*]
Drum. Enter LUCILIUS, PINDARUS, *and* SOLDIERS;
                enter BRUTUS *and* LUCIUS *from Brutus' tent*
BRUTUS Halt!
LUCILIUS Pass the word, "Halt!"
BRUTUS Well, now, Lucilius, is Cassius near?
LUCILIUS He is at hand, and Pindarus has come
    To bring you greetings from his master.   5
BRUTUS He sends a good man. Your master, Pindarus,
    Either by a change of heart or by bad officers
    Has given me sound reasons for wishing
    Things done were undone, but if he is at hand
    I shall have a personal explanation.   10
PINDARUS I do not doubt
    That my noble master will emerge,
    Such as he is, deserving of respect and honor.
BRUTUS No doubt.
    [*Aside to* LUCILIUS] A word with you, Lucilius.   15
    How were you received; let me be clear on that.
LUCILIUS With courtesy and adequate respect,
    But not with the usual familiarity,
    Nor with the free and friendly conversation,

As he hath used of old. 20

BRUTUS Thou hast described

A hot friend cooling. Ever note, Lucilius,

When love begins to sicken and decay

It useth an enforced ceremony.

There are no tricks in plain and simple faith; 25

But hollow men, like horses hot at hand,

Make gallant show and promise of their mettle.

Low march within.

But when they should endure the bloody spur,

They fall their crests, and like deceitful jades

Sink in the trial. Comes his army on? 30

LUCILIUS They mean this night in Sardis to be quartered.

The greater part, the horse in general,

Are come with Cassius.

Enter CASSIUS *and* SOLDIERS

BRUTUS Hark, he is arrived.

March gently on to meet him. 35

CASSIUS Stand ho!

BRUTUS Stand ho, speak the word along!

FIRST SOLDIER Stand!

SECOND SOLDIER Stand!

THIRD SOLDIER Stand! 40

CASSIUS Most noble brother, you have done me wrong.

BRUTUS Judge me, you gods! Wrong I mine enemies?

And if not so, how should I wrong a brother?

CASSIUS Brutus, this sober form of yours hides wrongs,

And when you do them— 45

That he used to have.   20

BRUTUS You have described

An ardent friendship cooling. Remember, Lucilius,

When love begins to sicken and decay,

It resorts to strained courtesy.

There are no tricks in sincere friendship;   25

But empty men, like horses raring to go,

Make a fine show and give promise of spirit.

The sound of marching.

But when they should respond to the spur,

They drop their heads, and like fickle women,

Fail the test. Is his army coming?   30

LUCILIUS They intend to make camp tonight at Sardis.

The larger body, mostly cavalry,

Have come with Cassius.

Enter CASSIUS *and* SOLDIERS

BRUTUS Listen, he has arrived.

March slowly to meet him.   35

CASSIUS Halt!

BRUTUS Halt! Pass the word along!

FIRST SOLDIER Halt!

SECOND SOLDIER Halt!

THIRD SOLDIER Halt!   40

CASSIUS Most noble brother, you have wronged me!

BRUTUS Judge me, you gods, do I even wrong my enemies?

And if not them, how could I wrong a brother?

CASSIUS Brutus, your dignified manner conceals your wrongs,

And when you commit them—   45

BRUTUS Cassius, be content,

    Speak your griefs softly, I do know you well.

    Before the eyes of both our armies here—

    Which should perceive nothing but love from us—

    Let us not wrangle. Bid them move away.   50

    Then in my tent, Cassius, enlarge your griefs

    And I will give you audience.

CASSIUS Pindarus,

    Bid our commanders lead their charges off

    A little from this ground.   55

BRUTUS Lucius, do you the like, and let no man

    Come to our tent till we have done our conference.

    Let Lucilius and Titinius guard our door.

                Exeunt all but BRUTUS *and* CASSIUS

Scene 3 [*In Brutus' tent*]

CASSIUS That you have wronged me doth appear in this:

    You have condemned and noted Lucius Pella

    For taking bribes here of the Sardians,

    Wherein my letters, praying on his side,

    Because I knew the man, was slighted off.   5

BRUTUS You have wronged yourself to write in such a case.

CASSIUS In such a time as this it is not meet

    That every nice offense should bear his comment.

BRUTUS Let me tell you, Cassius, you yourself

    Are much condemned to have an itching palm,   10

    To sell and mart your offices for gold

    To undeservers.

BRUTUS Cassius, keep calm,

    Speak your grievances quietly; I understand you well.

    In the presence of both our armies here—

    Which should see nothing but harmony between us—

    Let us not wrangle. Have them move away.   50

    Then in my tent, Cassius, set out your complaints in full,

    And I will listen to them.

CASSIUS Pindarus,

    Order our commanders to move their troops back

    A little from here.   55

BRUTUS Lucius, you do the same, and let no man

    Come to our tent till we have finished our conference.

    Lucilius and Titinius, guard our door.

                       Exit all but BRUTUS *and* CASSIUS

Scene 3 [*In Brutus' tent*]

CASSIUS That you have wronged me is clear by this:

    You have publicly disgraced Lucius Pella

    For taking bribes from the Sardians,

    And my letters, pleading on his behalf,

    Because I knew the man, have gone ignored.   5

BRUTUS You have put yourself in the wrong to support such a man.

CASSIUS In a time like this, it isn't proper

    That every small offense should be criticized.

BRUTUS Let me tell you, Cassius, you yourself are

    Often accused of having an itchy palm,   10

    Of selling and trading your appointments

    To worthless men.

CASSIUS I, an itching palm?

You know that you are Brutus that speaks this,

Or, by the gods, this speech were else your last.   15

BRUTUS The name of Cassius honors this corruption,

And chastisement doth therefore hide his head.

CASSIUS Chastisement?

BRUTUS Remember March, the ides of March remember:

Did not great Julius bleed for justice' sake?   20

What villain touched his body, that did stab

And not for justice? What, shall one of us,

That struck the foremost man of all this world,

But for supporting robbers, shall we now

Contaminate our fingers with base bribes   25

And sell the mighty space of our large honors

For so much trash as may be grasped thus?

I had rather be a dog and bay the moon

Than such a Roman.

CASSIUS Brutus, bait not me.   30

I'll not endure it. You forget yourself

To hedge me in. I am a soldier, I,

Older in practice, abler than yourself

To make conditions.

BRUTUS Go to, you are not, Cassius!   35

CASSIUS I am.

BRUTUS I say you are not.

CASSIUS Urge me no more, I shall forget myself.

Have mind upon your health, tempt me no farther!

BRUTUS Away, slight man!   40

CASSIUS I, an itchy palm?

> You know that only Brutus could speak this way
>
> Or, by the gods, this speech would be your last.   15

BRUTUS The name of Cassius sanctions this corruption,

> And so they are not punished.

CASSIUS Punished?

BRUTUS Remember March. Remember the ides of March.

> Did not the great Julius shed his blood for justice's sake?   20
>
> Who touched his body and was such a villain he did not stab
>
> For justice's sake? What, shall one of us,
>
> Who killed the foremost man in all the world
>
> Only because he supported robbers, shall we now
>
> Contaminate our fingers with mean bribes   25
>
> And sacrifice the high honors we have gained
>
> For so much rubbish as I can hold in my hand?
>
> I would rather be a dog and howl at the moon
>
> Than be such a Roman.

CASSIUS Brutus, don't provoke me.   30

> I won't stand for it. You forget yourself
>
> To restrict my actions. I am a soldier, I am
>
> More experienced and more capable than you
>
> At managing things.

BRUTUS Nonsense, you are not, Cassius!   35

CASSIUS I am.

BRUTUS I say you are not.

CASSIUS Don't provoke me further. I shall forget myself.

> Watch out for your health, if you try my patience.

BRUTUS Go away, little man!   40

CASSIUS Is 't possible?

BRUTUS Hear me, for I will speak.

    Must I give way and room to your rash choler?

    Shall I be frighted when a madman stares?

CASSIUS O ye gods, ye gods, must I endure all this?   45

BRUTUS All this? Ay, more. Fret till your proud heart break.

    Go show your slaves how choleric you are,

    And make your bondmen tremble. Must I budge?

    Must I observe you? Must I stand and crouch

    Under your testy humor? By the gods,   50

    You shall digest the venom of your spleen

    Though it do split you. For, from this day forth,

    I'll use you for my mirth, yea, for my laughter,

    When you are waspish.

CASSIUS Is it come to this?   55

BRUTUS You say you are a better soldier.

    Let it appear so, make your vaunting true,

    And it shall please me well. For mine own part

    I shall be glad to learn of noble men.

CASSIUS You wrong me every way, you wrong me, Brutus.   60

    I said an elder soldier, not a better,

    Did I say "better"?

BRUTUS If you did, I care not.

CASSIUS When Caesar lived, he durst not thus have moved me.

BRUTUS Peace, peace, you durst not so have tempted him.   65

CASSIUS I durst not?

BRUTUS No.

CASSIUS What? Durst not tempt him?

CASSIUS Is it possible?

BRUTUS Listen, for I'll be blunt.

    Must I submit and give free rein to your bad temper?

    Shall I be frightened when a madman stares?

CASSIUS Oh, you gods, you gods, must I endure all this?　　　45

BRUTUS All this? Yes, and more. Rage till your proud heart breaks.

    Go and show your slaves how angry you are,

    And make your captives tremble. Must I flinch?

    Must I humor you? Must I stand here and cringe

    Under your irritable temper? By the gods,　　　50

    You shall swallow the poison of your anger

    Even though you burst. For, from this day on,

    I'll amuse myself with you, yes, even laugh

    When you become vicious.

CASSIUS Has it come to this?　　　55

BRUTUS You say you are a better soldier.

    Then prove it, make your boasts come true,

    And I shall be well pleased. For my part,

    I am always glad to learn of noble men.

CASSIUS You wrong me in every way, you wrong me, Brutus.　　　60

    I said a more experienced soldier, not a better one.

    Did I say "better"?

BRUTUS Even if you did, I don't care.

CASSIUS When Caesar was alive, he dared not anger me like this.

BRUTUS Come, come, you wouldn't have dared provoke him.　　　65

CASSIUS Would not have dared?

BRUTUS No.

CASSIUS What? Dare not provoke him?

BRUTUS For your life you durst not.

CASSIUS Do not presume too much upon my love,   70
    I may do that I shall be sorry for.

BRUTUS You have done that you should be sorry for.
    There is no terror, Cassius, in your threats,
    For I am armed so strong in honesty
    That they pass by me as the idle wind,   75
    Which I respect not. I did send to you
    For certain sums of gold, which you denied me,
    For I can raise no money by vile means.
    By heaven, I had rather coin my heart
    And drop my blood for drachmas than to wring   80
    From the hard hands of peasants their vile trash
    By any indirection. I did send
    To you for gold to pay my legions,
    Which you denied me. Was that done like Cassius?
    Should I have answered Caius Cassius so?   85
    When Marcus Brutus grows so covetous
    To lock such rascal counters from his friends,
    Be ready, gods, with all your thunderbolts;
    Dash him to pieces!

CASSIUS I denied you not.   90

BRUTUS You did.

CASSIUS I did not. He was but a fool that brought
    My answer back. Brutus hath rived my heart.
    A friend should bear his friend's infirmities,
    But Brutus makes mine greater than they are.   95

BRUTUS I do not, till you practice them on me.

BRUTUS Not on your life did you dare.

CASSIUS Do not rely too much on my affection;   70

    I may do something I shall be sorry for.

BRUTUS You have already done what you should be sorry for.

    There is no terror, Cassius, in your threats,

    For I am armed so strong in integrity

    That they pass me by like an idle wind,   75

    To which I pay no attention. I asked you

    For certain sums of gold, and you denied me.

    I cannot raise money by dishonest means.

    By heaven, I would rather melt my heart for coins

    And turn my blood to drachmas than wring   80

    From the hard hands of peasants their small change

    By some crooked means. I asked

    You for gold to pay my legions,

    And you have turned me down. Was that the real Cassius?

    Would I have answered Caius Cassius like that?   85

    When Marcus Brutus grows so miserly

    As to deny some trashy coins to his friends,

    May the gods be ready with all their thunderbolts

    To dash him to pieces!

CASSIUS I didn't turn you down.   90

BRUTUS Yes, you did.

CASSIUS I did not. He was a fool that came

    Back with my answer. Brutus has broken my heart.

    A friend should bear with a friend's weaknesses,

    But Brutus makes mine greater than they are.   95

BRUTUS I do not, till you use them against me.

CASSIUS You love me not.

BRUTUS I do not like your faults.

CASSIUS A friendly eye could never see such faults.

BRUTUS A flatterer's eye would not, though they do appear   100
    As huge as high Olympus.

CASSIUS Come, Antony, and young Octavius, come,
    Revenge yourselves alone on Cassius,
    For Cassius is aweary of the world—
    Hated by one he loves, braved by his brother,   105
    Checked like a bondman, all his faults observed,
    Set in a notebook, learned, and conned by rote,
    To cast into my teeth. O, I could weep
    My spirit from mine eyes! There is my dagger
    And here my naked breast; within, a heart   110
    Dearer than Pluto's mine, richer than gold.
    If that thou beest a Roman take it forth,
    I that denied thee gold will give my heart.
    Strike as thou didst at Caesar. For I know
    When thou didst hate him worst, thou lovedst him better   115
    Than ever thou lovedst Cassius.

BRUTUS Sheathe your dagger.
    Be angry when you will, it shall have scope.
    Do what you will, dishonor shall be humor.
    O Cassius, you are yoked with a lamb   120
    That carries anger as the flint bears fire,
    Who, much enforced, shows a hasty spark
    And straight is cold again.

CASSIUS Hath Cassius lived

CASSIUS You are not my friend.

BRUTUS I do not like your faults.

CASSIUS A friend's eye would never see such faults.

BRUTUS A flatterer's eye would not, even though they appeared   100
   As huge as high Olympus.

CASSIUS Come, Antony, and young Octavius, come,
   And take your revenge on Cassius alone,
   For Cassius is weary of the world—
   Hated by one he admires, defied by his brother,   105
   Rebuked like a slave, all his faults analyzed,
   Set down in a notebook, learned, and recited by heart
   And thrown in his teeth. Oh, I could weep
   My life from my eyes! There is my dagger
   And here my naked breast. Within, is a heart   110
   More precious than Pluto's mine, richer than gold.
   If you are truly a Roman, cut it out;
   I, who denied you gold, will give you my heart.
   Strike as you did at Caesar. For I know that
   When you hated him most, you admired him more   115
   Than you ever have Cassius.

BRUTUS Put away your dagger.
   Get angry whenever you want, without restriction.
   Whatever you do, I'll assume your insults as a passing mood.
   Oh, Cassius, you are allied with a lamb,   120
   One who carries anger like a flint carries fire,
   Struck with force, it shows a hasty spark,
   And at once is cold again.

CASSIUS Has Cassius lived

To be but mirth and laughter to his Brutus   125

When grief and blood ill-tempered vexeth him?

BRUTUS When I spoke that, I was ill-tempered too.

CASSIUS Do you confess so much? Give me your hand.

BRUTUS And my heart too.

CASSIUS O Brutus!   130

BRUTUS What's the matter?

CASSIUS Have not you love enough to bear with me

When that rash humor which my mother gave me

Makes me forgetful?

BRUTUS Yes, Cassius, and from henceforth   135

When you are over-earnest with your Brutus,

He'll think your mother chides, and leave you so.

Enter a POET, *followed by* LUCILIUS, TITINIUS, *and* LUCIUS

POET Let me go in to see the generals.

There is some grudge between 'em, 'tis not meet

They be alone.   140

LUCILIUS You shall not come to them.

POET Nothing but death shall stay me.

CASSIUS How now, what's the matter?

POET For shame, you generals, what do you mean?

Love and be friends, as two such men should be,   145

For I have seen more years, I'm sure, than ye.

CASSIUS Ha, ha, how vilely doth this cynic rhyme!

BRUTUS Get you hence, sirrah; saucy fellow, hence!

CASSIUS Bear with him, Brutus, 'tis his fashion.

BRUTUS I'll know his humor when he knows his time.   150

What should the wars do with these jigging fools?

His life only to be a source of laughter to Brutus,   125

When grief and bad temper take hold of him?

BRUTUS When I said that, I was ill-tempered too.

CASSIUS Do you admit that? Give me your hand.

BRUTUS And my heart too.

CASSIUS Oh, Brutus!   130

BRUTUS What's the matter?

CASSIUS Don't you have love enough to put up with me

When that rash temper I inherited from my mother

Makes me forget myself?

BRUTUS Yes, Cassius, and from now on   135

When you are too severe with your Brutus,

He'll think it's your mother who scolds, and leave it at that.

    Enter a POET, *followed by* LUCILIUS, TITINIUS, *and* LUCIUS

POET Let me in to see the generals.

There is some ill-feeling between them, and it's not fitting

That they are left alone.   140

LUCILIUS You cannot go in.

POET Nothing short of death will prevent me.

CASSIUS Well, now, what's the matter?

POET Shame on you, generals! What are you up to?

Love and be friends, as such men were meant to,   145

For I have seen more years, I'm sure, than you two.

CASSIUS Ha, ha, what a bad poet he is!

BRUTUS Get out of here, sir; rude fellow, go!

CASSIUS Put up with him, Brutus. It's just his manner.

BRUTUS I'll allow for his manners when he learns the right time.   150

What use in war are these rhyming fools?

Companion, hence!

CASSIUS   Away, away, be gone!

Exit POET

BRUTUS   Lucilius and Titinius, bid the commanders

Prepare to lodge their companies tonight.   155

CASSIUS   And come yourselves, and bring Messala with you

Immediately to us.

Exeunt LUCILIUS *and* TITINIUS

BRUTUS   [*To* LUCIUS *within*] Lucius, a bowl of wine!

CASSIUS   I did not think you could have been so angry.

BRUTUS   O Cassius, I am sick of many griefs.   160

CASSIUS   Of your philosophy you make no use

If you give place to accidental evils.

BRUTUS   No man bears sorrow better. Portia is dead.

CASSIUS   Ha? Portia?

BRUTUS   She is dead.   165

CASSIUS   How 'scaped I killing when I crossed you so?

O insupportable and touching loss!

Upon what sickness?

BRUTUS   Impatient of my absence,

And grief that young Octavius with Mark Antony   170

Have made themselves so strong—for with her death

That tidings came. With this she fell distract

And, her attendants absent, swallowed fire.

CASSIUS   And died so?

BRUTUS   Even so.   175

CASSIUS   O ye immortal gods!

Enter LUCIUS *with wine and candles*

Friend, go away!

CASSIUS Away, away, get going!

Exit POET

BRUTUS Lucilius and Titinius, order the commanders

To prepare to set up camp for the night.   155

CASSIUS And come yourselves, and bring Messala

To us immediately.

Exit LUCILIUS *and* TITINIUS

BRUTUS [*To* LUCIUS *within*] Lucius, a bowl of wine!

CASSIUS I never thought you could be so angry.

BRUTUS Oh, Cassius, I am afflicted with many sorrows.   160

CASSIUS You aren't using your philosophy

If you give in to chance evils.

BRUTUS No man bears sorrow better. Portia is dead.

CASSIUS What? Portia?

BRUTUS She is dead.   165

CASSIUS How did I escape being killed when I opposed you?

Oh, unbearable and touching loss!

What did she die of?

BRUTUS Unable to endure my absence,

And upset that young Octavius and Mark Antony   170

Had become allies—news of that

Came with her death—with this she became distraught

And, when left unattended, put burning coals in her mouth.

CASSIUS And then she died?

BRUTUS Even so.   175

CASSIUS Oh, immortal gods!

Enter LUCIUS *with wine and candles*

BRUTUS Speak no more of her. Give me a bowl of wine.

In this I bury all unkindness, Cassius. [*Drinks*]

CASSIUS My heart is thirsty for that noble pledge.

Fill, Lucius, till the wine o'erswell the cup,　　　　　　180

I cannot drink too much of Brutus' love. [*Drinks*]

Exit LUCIUS

Enter TITINIUS *and* MESSALA

BRUTUS Come in, Titinius; welcome, good Messala.

Now sit we close about this taper here

And call in question our necessities.

CASSIUS Portia, art thou gone?　　　　　　185

BRUTUS No more, I pray you.

Messala, I have received letters

That young Octavius and Mark Antony

Come down upon us with a mighty power,

Bending their expedition toward Philippi.　　　　　　190

MESSALA Myself have letters of the selfsame tenor.

BRUTUS With what addition?

MESSALA That by proscription and bills of outlawry

Octavius, Antony, and Lepidus

Have put to death an hundred senators.　　　　　　195

BRUTUS Therein our letters do not well agree.

Mine speak of seventy senators that died

By their proscriptions, Cicero being one.

CASSIUS Cicero one?

MESSALA Cicero is dead,　　　　　　200

And by that order of proscription.

Had you your letters from your wife, my lord?

BRUTUS Let's talk no more of her. Give me a bowl of wine.

In this I drown all the malice between us, Cassius. [*Drinks*]

CASSIUS My heart thirsts for that noble pledge.

Lucius, fill the wine till it overflows my cup,   180

I cannot drink too much of Brutus' love. [*Drinks*]

Exit LUCIUS

Enter TITINIUS *and* MESSALA

BRUTUS Come in Titinius; welcome, good Messala.

Let's sit around this candle here

And inquire what needs to be done.

CASSIUS Portia, are you dead?   185

BRUTUS No more, please.

Messala, I have letters saying

That young Octavius and Mark Antony

Come toward us with a mighty force,

Directing their advance toward Philippi.   190

MESSALA I have letters to the same effect.

BRUTUS With anything further?

MESSALA That by sentence of death and lists of banishment

Octavius, Antony, and Lepidus

Have put to death one hundred senators.   195

BRUTUS In that respect our letters do not agree.

Mine speak of seventy senators that died

By their sentence, Cicero being one.

CASSIUS Cicero was one?

MESSALA Cicero is dead   200

By order of that sentence.

Have you had letters from your wife, my lord?

BRUTUS No, Messala.

MESSALA Nor nothing in your letters writ of her?

BRUTUS Nothing, Messala.   205

MESSALA That, methinks, is strange.

BRUTUS Why ask you? Hear you aught of her in yours?

MESSALA No, my lord.

BRUTUS Now as you are a Roman tell me true.

MESSALA Then like a Roman bear the truth I tell,   210

  For certain she is dead, and by strange manner.

BRUTUS Why, farewell, Portia. We must die, Messala.

  With meditating that she must die once,

  I have the patience to endure it now.

MESSALA Even so, great men great losses should endure.   215

CASSIUS I have had as much of this in art as you,

  But yet my nature could not bear it so.

BRUTUS Well, to our work alive. What do you think

  Of marching to Philippi presently?

CASSIUS I do not think it good.   220

BRUTUS Your reason?

CASSIUS This it is:

  'Tis better that the enemy seek us,

  So shall he waste his means, weary his soldiers,

  Doing himself offense, whilst we, lying still,   225

  Are full of rest, defense, and nimbleness.

BRUTUS Good reasons must of force give place to better.

  The people 'twixt Philippi and this ground

  Do stand but in forced affection,

  For they have grudged us contribution.   230

BRUTUS No, Messala.

MESSALA Nor nothing in your letters about her?

BRUTUS Nothing, Messala.   205

MESSALA I think that's strange.

BRUTUS Why do you ask? Have you heard of her in yours?

MESSALA No, my lord.

BRUTUS Now as a Roman, tell me the truth.

MESSALA Then, like a Roman, be prepared to bear it.   210

    It is certain she is dead, and died in a strange way.

BRUTUS Why, farewell, Portia. We all must die, Messala.

    Thinking that she can die only once,

    I have the courage to endure it now.

MESSALA This is how great men suffer great losses.   215

CASSIUS I have in theory as much strength as you,

    But I couldn't bear news like that.

BRUTUS We're still alive, let's get to work. What do you think

    Of marching to Philippi immediately?

CASSIUS I do not think it is a good idea.   220

BRUTUS Your reason?

CASSIUS It's this.

    It is better that the enemy seek us.

    In this way, he'll waste his resources, tire his soldiers,

    Harm himself, while we, lying still,   225

    Will be rested, fresh, and alert.

BRUTUS Good reasons must give way to better ones.

    The people between Philippi and here

    Are friendly only because they have to be;

    They have begrudged us supplies.   230

The enemy, marching along by them,

By them shall make a fuller number up,

Come on refreshed, new added, and encouraged,

From which advantage shall we cut him off

If at Philippi we do face him there,   235

These people at our back.

CASSIUS Hear me, good brother—

BRUTUS Under your pardon. You must note beside

That we have tried the utmost of our friends,

Our legions are brimful, our cause is ripe.   240

The enemy increaseth every day;

We, at the height, are ready to decline.

There is a tide in the affairs of men

Which, taken at the flood, leads on to fortune;

Omitted, all the voyage of their life   245

Is bound in shallows and in miseries.

On such a full sea are we now afloat,

And we must take the current when it serves

Or lose our ventures.

CASSIUS Then, with your will, go on,   250

We'll along ourselves and meet them at Philippi.

BRUTUS The deep of night is crept upon our talk,

And nature must obey necessity,

Which we will niggard with a little rest.

There is no more to say.   255

CASSIUS No more. Good night.

Early tomorrow will we rise and hence.

BRUTUS Lucius!

The enemy, marching among them,

Shall increase the number of their troops,

Arrive refreshed, reinforced, with spirits high.

We will cut him off from this advantage

If we can face him at Philippi,   235

With these people behind us.

CASSIUS Hear me, good brother—

BRUTUS I beg your pardon. You must also consider

That we have strained our friends' resources to the limit,

Our legions are full strength, our cause is at its peak.   240

The enemy grows stronger every day;

We, at the height of our fortunes, are ready to decline.

There is a time in the affairs of men

That, taken at high tide, leads on to fortune;

Neglected, all the voyage of their life   245

Is bound in shallow water and in misery.

On such a full sea are we now afloat,

And we must use the tide when it favors us,

Or lose what we have risked.

CASSIUS Then, as you wish, go on.   250

We'll do the same and meet them at Philippi.

BRUTUS Night has come as we talked,

And nature now demands

That we will take a little rest.

There is no more to say.   255

CASSIUS No more. Good night.

Early tomorrow we'll rise and set off.

BRUTUS Lucius!

Enter LUCIUS

My gown.

Exit LUCIUS

Farewell, good Messala.   260

Good night, Titinius. Noble, noble Cassius,

Good night and good repose.

CASSIUS   O my dear brother!

This was an ill beginning of the night.

Never come such division 'tween our souls!   265

Let it not, Brutus.

Enter LUCIUS *with the gown*

BRUTUS   Everything is well.

CASSIUS   Good night, my lord.

BRUTUS   Good night, good brother.

TITINIUS and MESSALA   Good night, Lord Brutus.   270

BRUTUS   Farewell every one.

Exeunt all but BRUTUS *and* LUCIUS

Give me the gown. Where is thy instrument?

LUCIUS   Here in the tent.

BRUTUS   What, thou speak'st drowsily?

Poor knave, I blame thee not, thou are o'erwatched.   275

Call Claudius and some other of my men,

I'll have them sleep on cushions in my tent.

LUCIUS   Varro and Claudius!

Enter VARRO *and* CLAUDIUS

VARRO   Calls my lord?

BRUTUS   I pray you, sirs, lie in my tent and sleep,   280

Enter LUCIUS

Get me my gown.

Exit LUCIUS

Farewell, good Messala.   260

Good night, Titinius. Noble, noble Cassius,

Good night and sleep well.

CASSIUS   Oh, my dear brother!

This was a bad beginning for the evening.

May we never have such a division as that!   265

Don't let it happen, Brutus.

Enter LUCIUS *with the gown*

BRUTUS   Everything's fine.

CASSIUS   Good night, my lord.

BRUTUS   Good night, good brother.

TITINIUS and MESSALA   Good night, Lord Brutus.   270

BRUTUS   Farewell, everyone.

Exit all but BRUTUS *and* LUCIUS

Give me the gown. Where is your lute?

LUCIUS   Somewhere in the tent.

BRUTUS   What, you sound sleepy.

Poor boy, I don't blame you, you are up too late.   275

Call Claudius and some other men of mine.

I'll have them sleep on cushions in my tent.

LUCIUS   Varro and Claudius!

Enter VARRO *and* CLAUDIUS

VARRO   You called, my lord?

BRUTUS   I ask you, sirs, to lie in my tent and sleep.   280

It may be I shall raise you up by and by

On business to my brother Cassius.

VARRO So please you, we will stand and watch your pleasure.

BRUTUS I will not have it so. Lie down, good sirs,

It may be I shall otherwise bethink me.   285

Look, Lucius, here's the book I sought for so,

I put it in the pocket of my gown.

LUCIUS I was sure your lordship did not give it me.

BRUTUS Bear with me, good boy, I am much forgetful.

Canst thou hold up thy heavy eyes awhile   290

And touch thy instrument a strain or two?

LUCIUS Ay, my lord, an 't please you.

BRUTUS It does, my boy.

I trouble thee too much, but thou art willing.

LUCIUS It is my duty, sir.   295

BRUTUS I should not urge thy duty past thy might,

I know young bloods look for a time of rest.

LUCIUS I have slept, my lord, already.

BRUTUS It was well done and thou shalt sleep again,

I will not hold thee long. If I do live   300

I will be good to thee.

Music, song. [LUCIUS *falls asleep.*]

This is a sleepy tune. O murd'rous slumber,

Layest thou thy leaden mace upon my boy,

That plays thee music? Gentle knave, good night,

I will not do thee so much wrong to wake thee.   305

If thou dost nod thou break'st thy instrument.

I'll take it from thee and, good boy, good night.

I might wake you up later

To go on business to my brother Cassius.

VARRO If it's all the same, we'll stay awake for your wishes.

BRUTUS That I will not allow. Lie down, good sirs.

It may be that I shall change my mind.   285

Look, Lucius, here's the book I was searching for.

I put it in the pocket of my gown.

LUCIUS I was sure your lordship hadn't given it to me.

BRUTUS Be patient with me, boy, I'm getting forgetful.

Can you keep your eyes open for awhile   290

And play a melody or two?

LUCIUS Yes, my lord, if it pleases you.

BRUTUS It does, my boy.

I trouble you too much, but you are willing.

LUCIUS It is my duty, sir.   295

BRUTUS I should not press your duty past your strength,

I know young people require time for rest.

LUCIUS I have slept already, my lord.

BRUTUS It was a good idea, and you shall sleep again.

I won't keep you long. If I survive,   300

I will be good to you.

Music, song. [LUCIUS *falls asleep.*]

That was a sleepy tune. Oh, murderous sleep,

Have you touched my boy with your leaden wand

When he plays you music? Gentle boy, good night,

I won't be so cruel as to wake you.   305

If you nod, you'll break your lute.

I'll take it from you and, good boy, good night.

Let me see, let me see, is not the leaf turned down
Where I left reading? Here it is, I think.

Enter the GHOST *of* CAESAR

How ill this taper burns! Ha, who comes here?   310
I think it is the weakness of mine eyes
That shapes this monstrous apparition.
It comes upon me. Are thou any thing?
Art thou some god, some angel, or some devil,
That mak'st my blood run cold and my hair to stare?   315
Speak to me what thou art.

GHOST   Thy evil spirit, Brutus.

BRUTUS   Why com'st thou?

GHOST   To tell thee thou shalt see me at Philippi.

BRUTUS   Well, then I shall see thee again?   320

GHOST   Ay, at Philippi.

BRUTUS   Why, I will see thee at Philippi then.

Exit GHOST

Now I have taken heart thou vanishest.
Ill spirit, I would hold more talk with thee,
Boy, Lucius! Varro! Claudius, sirs, awake!   325
Claudius!

LUCIUS   The strings, my lord, are false.

BRUTUS   He thinks he still is at his instrument.
Lucius, awake!

LUCIUS   My lord?   330

BRUTUS   Didst thou dream, Lucius, that thou so cried'st out?

LUCIUS   My lord, I do not know that I did cry.

BRUTUS   Yes, that thou didst. Didst thou see anything?

Let me see, let me see, isn't the page turned down
Where I left off reading? Here it is, I think.

Enter the GHOST *of* CAESAR

How dimly this candle burns! What, who is that?   310
I think it is the weakness of my eyes
That causes this unnatural apparition.
It comes toward me. Are you real?
Are you some god, some angel, or some devil
That makes my blood run cold and my hair stand on end?   315
Tell me what you are.

GHOST   Your evil spirit, Brutus.

BRUTUS   Why are you here?

GHOST   To tell you that you shall see me at Philippi.

BRUTUS   Well, then I shall see you again?   320

GHOST   Yes, at Philippi.

BRUTUS   Why, I will see you at Philippi then.

Exit GHOST

Now I have my courage back, you vanish.
Evil spirit, I would talk longer with you.
Boy, Lucius! Varro! Claudius! Sirs, awake!   325
Claudius!

LUCIUS   The strings, my lord, are out of tune.

BRUTUS   He thinks he's still playing his instrument.
Lucius, wake up!

LUCIUS   My lord?   330

BRUTUS   Was it a dream, Lucius, that caused you to cry out?

LUCIUS   My lord, I don't think I cried out.

BRUTUS   Yes, you did. Did you see anything?

LUCIUS Nothing, my lord.

BRUTUS Sleep again, Lucius. Sirrah Claudius!   335

    [*To* VARRO] Fellow, thou, awake!

VARRO My lord?

CLAUDIUS My lord?

BRUTUS Why did you cry out, sirs, in your sleep?

BOTH Did we, my lord?   340

BRUTUS Ay. Saw you anything?

VARRO No, my lord, I saw nothing.

CLAUDIUS Nor I, my lord.

BRUTUS Go and commend me to my brother Cassius.

    Bid him set on his powers betimes before,   345

    And we will follow.

BOTH It shall be done, my lord.

                          Exeunt

LUCIUS Nothing, my lord.

BRUTUS Sleep again, Lucius. You there, Claudius!   335

  [*To* VARRO] Fellow, you, wake up!

VARRO My lord?

CLAUDIUS My lord?

BRUTUS Why did you cry out, sirs, in your sleep?

BOTH Did we, my lord?   340

BRUTUS Yes. Did you see anything?

VARRO No, my lord, I saw nothing.

CLAUDIUS Nor I, my lord.

BRUTUS Go and greet my brother Cassius.

  Ask him to order his forces to advance early,   345

  And we will follow.

BOTH It shall be done, my lord.

                          They exit

Act Five

Scene 1 [*The battlefield at Philippi in Greece*]

                Enter OCTAVIUS, ANTONY, *and their* ARMY

OCTAVIUS Now, Antony, our hopes are answered.

    You said the enemy would not come down

    But keep the hills and upper regions.

    It proves not so; their battles are at hand,

    They mean to warn us at Philippi here,   5

    Answering before we do demand of them.

ANTONY Tut, I am in their bosoms, and I know

    Wherefore they do it. They could be content

    To visit other places and come down

    With fearful bravery, thinking by this face   10

    To fasten in our thoughts that they have courage.

    But 'tis not so

                  Enter a MESSENGER

MESSENGER Prepare you, generals,

    The enemy comes on in gallant show,

    Their bloody sign of battle is hung out,   15

    And something to be done immediately.

ANTONY Octavius, lead your battle softly on

    Upon the left hand of the even field.

OCTAVIUS Upon the right hand I, keep thou the left.

ANTONY Why do you cross me in this exigent?   20

OCTAVIUS I do not cross you, but I will do so.

Drum, beating a march. Enter BRUTUS, CASSIUS, *and their* ARMY

BRUTUS They stand and would have parley.

Act Five

Scene 1 [*The battlefield at Philippi in Greece*]

Enter OCTAVIUS, ANTONY, *and their* ARMY

OCTAVIUS Now, Antony, our hopes are answered.

    You said the enemy would not come down

    But stay in the hills and on higher ground.

    This is not the case; their armies are at hand.

    They mean to challenge us here at Philippi,   5

    Responding to our threat before we have issued it.

ANTONY Oh, come, I can read their thoughts, and I know

    Why they do what they do. They would rather meet us

    In another place but come down here,

    Full of bravado, thinking by this appearance   10

    To convince us that they have courage.

    But it's not so.

Enter a MESSENGER

MESSENGER Prepare yourselves, generals,

    The enemy comes toward us in a magnificent display,

    The red flag of battle is flying,   15

    And we must act immediately.

ANTONY Octavius, lead your army slowly

    On the left side on the level ground.

OCTAVIUS I will take the right side. You take the left.

ANTONY Why do you oppose me in this crisis?   20

OCTAVIUS I don't oppose you, but I will take the right.

Drum, beating a march. Enter BRUTUS, CASSIUS, *and their* ARMY

BRUTUS They've halted and want a conference.

CASSIUS Stand fast, Titinius, we must out and talk.

OCTAVIUS Mark Antony, shall we give sign of battle?

ANTONY No, Caesar, we will answer on their charge.   25

    Make forth, the generals would have some words.

OCTAVIUS Stir not until the signal.

BRUTUS Words before blows; is it so, countrymen?

OCTAVIUS Not that we love words better, as you do.

BRUTUS Good words are better than bad strokes, Octavius.   30

ANTONY In your bad strokes, Brutus, you give good words.

    Witness the hole you made in Caesar's heart,

    Crying, "Long live, hail, Caesar!"

CASSIUS Antony,

    The posture of your blows are as yet unknown;   35

    But for your words, they rob the Hybla bees

    And leave them honeyless.

ANTONY Not stingless too?

BRUTUS O yes, and soundless too,

    For you have stolen their buzzing, Antony,   40

    And very wisely threat before you sting.

ANTONY Villains! You did not so when your vile daggers

    Hacked one another in the sides of Caesar.

    You showed your teeth like apes and fawned like hounds,

    And bowed like bondmen, kissing Caesar's feet,   45

    Whilst damned Casca, like a cur, behind

    Struck Caesar on the neck. O you flatterers!

CASSIUS Flatterers? Now, Brutus, thank yourself.

    This tongue had not offended so today

    If Cassius might have ruled.   50

CASSIUS Halt, Titinius, we must leave the ranks and talk.

OCTAVIUS Mark Antony, shall we give the signal for battle?

ANTONY No, Caesar, we will counter their attack.   25

    Go forward. The generals want to talk.

OCTAVIUS Don't move until the signal.

BRUTUS Words before blows; is that it, countrymen?

OCTAVIUS It's not that we love words more, as you do.

BRUTUS Good words are better than bad swords, Octavius.   30

ANTONY In your bad sword, Brutus, you give good words:

    Witness the hole you made in Caesar's heart,

    At the same time, crying, "Long live, hail, Caesar."

CASSIUS Antony,

    How well you use your sword is yet unknown: 35

    As for your words, they rob the bees of Hybla

    And leave them honeyless.

ANTONY And stingless too?

BRUTUS Oh yes, and soundless too,

    For you have their buzzes, Antony,   40

    And wisely threaten before you sting.

ANTONY Villains! You gave no warning when your vile daggers

    Hacked one another in the body of Caesar.

    You grinned like apes and fawned like dogs,

    And bowed like slaves, kissing Caesar's feet,   45

    While damned Casca, like a mongrel, from behind

    Struck Caesar in the neck. Oh, you flatterers!

CASSIUS Flatterers? Now, Brutus, you have yourself to blame.

    This tongue would not be abusing us today

    If you had followed the advice of Cassius.   50

OCTAVIUS   Come, come, the cause. If arguing make us sweat,

The proof of it will turn to redder drops.

Look,

I draw a sword against conspirators;

When think you that the sword goes up again?   55

Never, till Caesar's three and thirty wounds

Be well avenged, or till another Caesar

Have added slaughter to the sword of traitors.

BRUTUS   Caesar, thou canst not die by traitors' hands

Unless thou bring'st them with thee.   60

OCTAVIUS   So I hope.

I was not born to die on Brutus' sword.

BRUTUS   O, if thou wert the noblest of thy strain,

Young man, thou couldst not die more honorable.

CASSIUS   A peevish schoolboy, worthless of such honor,   65

Joined with a masker and a reveller!

ANTONY   Old Cassius still!

OCTAVIUS   Come, Antony, away!

Defiance, traitors, hurl we in your teeth.

If you dare fight today, come to the field;   70

If not, when you have stomachs.

> *Exeunt* OCTAVIUS, ANTONY, *and* ARMY

CASSIUS   Why now, blow wind, swell billow, and swim bark!

The storm is up, and all is on the hazard.

BRUTUS   Ho, Lucilius, hark, a word with you.

LUCILIUS   My lord.   75

[BRUTUS *and* LUCILIUS *talk apart*]

OCTAVIUS Come, let's get to the point. Deciding the argument

    In battle will turn drops of sweat into drops of blood.

    Look,

    I draw my sword against the conspirators.

    When do you think I'll put it back again?   55

    Never, not till Caesar's three and thirty wounds

    Have been avenged, or till I, another Caesar,

    Have been added to the slaughter by the traitors.

BRUTUS Caesar, you cannot die by traitors' hands,

    Unless you've brought them with you.   60

OCTAVIUS So I hope.

    I was not born to die by Brutus' sword.

BRUTUS Oh, if you were the best of your noble breed,

    Young man, you could not die more honorably.

CASSIUS A childish schoolboy, unworthy of such honor,   65

    Allied with a party goer and a playboy.

ANTONY The same old Cassius.

OCTAVIUS Come, Antony, let's go!

    We hurl defiance, traitors, in your teeth.

    If you dare fight today, come to the field;   70

    If not now, come when you have the stomach.

                         Exit OCTAVIUS, ANTONY, *and* ARMY

CASSIUS Now, let the wind blow, the sails swell, and the ship swim!

    A storm is up, and all is at risk.

BRUTUS Lucilius, listen, I'd like a word with you.

LUCILIUS My lord.   75

[BRUTUS *and* LUCILIUS *talk privately*]

CASSIUS Messala!

MESSALA What says my general?

CASSIUS Messala,

> This is my birthday, as this very day
>
> Was Cassius born. Give me thy hand, Messala.   80
>
> Be thou witness that against my will
>
> (As Pompey was) am I compelled to set
>
> Upon one battle all our liberties.
>
> You know that I held Epicurus strong
>
> And his opinion. Now I change my mind   85
>
> And partly credit things that do presage.
>
> Coming from Sardis, on our former ensign
>
> Two mighty eagles fell, and there they perched,
>
> Gorging and feeding from our soldiers' hands,
>
> Who to Philippi here consorted us.   90
>
> This morning are they fled away and gone,
>
> And in their steads do ravens, crows, and kites
>
> Fly o'er our heads and downward look on us
>
> As we were sickly prey. Their shadows seem
>
> A canopy most fatal under which   95
>
> Our army lies, ready to give up the ghost.

MESSALA Believe not so.

CASSIUS I but believe it partly,

> For I am fresh of spirit and resolved
>
> To meet all perils very constantly.   100

BRUTUS [*Finishing his talk*] Even so, Lucilius.

CASSIUS Now, most noble Brutus,

> The gods today stand friendly that we may,

CASSIUS Messala!

MESSALA What does my general want?

CASSIUS Messala,

 This is my birthday, on this very day

 Was Cassius born. Give me your hand, Messala.   80

 Be my witness that against my will

 I am compelled, just as Pompey was, to stake

 All our liberties upon one battle.

 You know that I was once a follower of Epicurus

 And his philosophy. Now I have changed my mind   85

 And partly believe in things that foretell the future.

 Coming from Sardis, two mighty eagles landed

 On our highest banners and perched there,

 Gorging and feeding from our soldiers' hands,

 Accompanying us all the way to Philippi.   90

 This morning, they flew away and are gone,

 And in their place are ravens, crows, and hawks,

 Flying over our heads, looking down on us

 As though we were sick prey. Their shadows seem

 A funeral canopy under which   95

 Our army lies, ready to give up the ghost.

MESSALA Don't believe it.

CASSIUS I only half believe it,

 For I am cheerful in mind and ready

 To meet all dangers resolutely.   100

BRUTUS [*Finishing his talk*] Yes, indeed, Lucilius.

CASSIUS Now, most noble Brutus,

 May the gods be firm in their support so that we may,

Lovers in peace, lead on our days to age!
But since the affairs of men rests still incertain,   105
Let's reason with the worst that may befall.
If we do lose this battle, then is this
The very last time we shall speak together.
What are you then determined to do?
BRUTUS Even by the rule of that philosophy   110
By which I did blame Cato for the death
Which he did give himself—I know not how,
But I do find it cowardly and vile,
For fear of what might fall, so to prevent
The time of life—arming myself with patience   115
To stay the providence of some high powers
That govern us below.
CASSIUS Then if we lose this battle,
You are contented to be led in triumph
Through the streets of Rome?   120
BRUTUS No, Cassius, no. Think not, thou noble Roman,
That ever Brutus will go bound to Rome.
He bears too great a mind. But this same day
Must end that work the ides of March begun.
And whether we shall meet again I know not,   125
Therefore our everlasting farewell take:
For ever and for ever, farewell, Cassius!
If we do meet again, why, we shall smile;
If not, why then this parting was well made.
CASSIUS Why then, lead on. O, that a man might know   130
The end of this day's business ere it come!

As close friends, live to an old age.

But since the affairs of men always remain uncertain   105

Let us consider what to do if the worst should happen.

If we lose this battle, then this is

The very last time we shall speak together.

What have you then decided to do?

BRUTUS Following a certain rule of philosophy   110

That even leads me to blame Cato for

His suicide—I don't know why,

But I find it cowardly and vile,

Out of fear of what might happen, to cut

Life short. I will arm myself with patience   115

And await the fate destined by the high powers

That govern us here below.

CASSIUS Then if we lose this battle,

You will be content to be led in triumph

Through the streets of Rome?   120

BRUTUS No, Cassius, no. Do not think, noble Roman,

That Brutus will ever go in chains to Rome.

His nature is too noble for that. But this very day

Must end the work begun on the ides of March.

Whether we shall meet again, I do not know.   125

Therefore, let's take an everlasting farewell.

Forever and forever, farewell, Cassius!

If we do meet again, why, we shall smile;

If not, then this parting was well made.

CASSIUS Well, then, lead on. Oh, that a man might know   130

How this day will end before the end is known!

But it sufficeth that the day will end,

And then the end is known. Come ho, away.

Exeunt

Scene 2   [*The battlefield at Philippi*]

                Alarum. Enter BRUTUS *and* MESSALA

BRUTUS Ride, ride, Messala, ride, and give these bills

    Unto the legions on the other side.

Loud alarum

    Let them set on at once; for I perceive

    But cold demeanor in Octavius' wing,

    And sudden push gives them the overthrow.   5

    Ride, ride, Messala, let them all come down.

Exeunt

Scene 3   [*A hill overlooking the battlefield*]

               Alarums. Enter CASSIUS *and* TITINIUS

CASSIUS   O, look, Titinius, look, the villains fly!

    Myself have to mine own turned enemy.

    This ensign here of mine was turning back;

    I slew the coward and did take it from him.

TITINIUS   O Cassius, Brutus gave the word too early,   5

    Who, having some advantage on Octavius,

    Took it too eagerly. His soldiers fell to spoil

    Whilst we by Antony are all enclosed.

               Enter PINDARUS

PINDARUS   Fly further off, my lord, fly further off!

    Mark Antony is in your tents, my lord,   10

But it is enough that the day will end,

And then the end is known. Come, away.

They exit

Scene 2 [*The battlefield at Philippi*]

Sounds of battle. Enter BRUTUS *and* MESSALA

BRUTUS Ride, ride, Messala, ride, and give these orders

To the legions on the other side.

Loud sounds of battle.

Let them attack at once, for I notice

A lack of courage in Octavius' flank,

And a sudden push will overrun them.   5

Ride, ride, Messala, let them all attack.

They exit

Scene 3 [*A hill overlooking the battlefield*]

Sounds of battle. Enter CASSIUS *and* TITINIUS

CASSIUS Oh, look, Titinius, the villains run away!

I have turned against my own men.

My standard-bearer here was running away;

I killed the coward and took the flag from him.

TITINIUS Oh, Cassius, Brutus gave the word too early.   5

Having a slight advantage over Octavius,

He moved too quickly. His soldiers started looting

While we were surrounded by Antony's troops.

Enter PINDARUS

PINDARUS Retreat, my lord, fly further off!

Mark Antony has reached your camp, my lord,   10

Fly therefore, noble Cassius, fly far off.

CASSIUS This hill is far enough. Look, look, Titinius,

    Are those my tents where I perceive the fire?

TITINIUS They are, my lord.

CASSIUS Titinius, if thou lovest me,   15

    Mount thou my horse and hide thy spurs in him

    Till he have brought thee up to yonder troops

    And here again that I may rest assured

    Whether yond troops are friend or enemy.

TITINIUS I will be here again even with a thought.   20

                                     Exit

CASSIUS Go, Pindarus, get higher on that hill,

    My sight was ever thick. Regard Titinius

    And tell me what thou not'st about the field.

                          [*Exit* PINDARUS]

    This day I breathed first, time is come round

    And where I did begin, there shall I end;   25

    My life is run his compass. Sirrah, what news?

PINDARUS [*From the hill*] O my lord!

CASSIUS What news?

PINDARUS Titinius is enclosed round about

    With horsemen that make to him on the spur,   30

    Yet he spurs on. Now they are almost on him.

    Now Titinius! Now some light. O, he lights too.

    He's ta'en.

Shout.

    And hark, they shout for joy.

CASSIUS Come down, behold no more.   35

Therefore retreat, noble Cassius, fly further off!

CASSIUS This hill is far enough. Look, look, Titinius,

Are those my tents on fire?

TITINIUS They are, my lord.

CASSIUS Titinius, as you are my friend,   15

Mount my horse and dig your spurs into him

Till he has brought you to those distant troops

And then come back so that I may rest assured

Whether they are friend or enemy.

TITINIUS I will return with the speed of thought.   20

Exit

CASSIUS Go, Pindarus, climb higher on that hill,

My sight was never good, look for Titinius.

And tell me what you note on the battlefield.

[*Exit* PINDARUS]

This is the day I breathed my first; time has come round,

And where I began, there shall I end.   25

My life has come full circle. Fellow, what's happening?

PINDARUS [*From the hill*] Oh, my lord!

CASSIUS What's happening?

PINDARUS Titinius is encircled

By cavalry who race toward him,   30

Yet he races on. Now they are almost on him.

Now Titinius! Now some dismount. Oh, he dismounts too.

He's captured.

Shout.

And listen, they shout for joy.

CASSIUS Come down, look no more.   35

187

O, coward that I am to live so long
To see my best friend ta'en before my face.

Enter PINDARUS

Come hither, sirrah.
In Parthia did I take thee prisoner,
And then I swore thee, saving thy life,   40
That whatsoever I did bid thee do
Thou shouldst attempt it. Come now, keep thine oath.
Now be a freeman, and with this good sword,
That ran through Caesar's bowels, search this bosom.
Stand not to answer; here, take thou the hilts   45
And when my face is covered, as 'tis now,
Guide thou the sword. [PINDARUS *stabs him*]
Caesar, thou art revenged
Even with the sword that killed thee. [*Dies*]

PINDARUS   So I am free, yet would not so have been   50
Durst I have done my will. O Cassius,
Far from this country shall Pindarus run,
Where never Roman shall take note of him.

Exits

Enter TITINIUS *and* MESSALA

MESSALA   It is but change, Titinius, for Octavius
Is overthrown by noble Brutus' power,   55
As Cassius' legions are by Antony.

TITINIUS   These tidings will well comfort Cassius.

MESSALA   Where did you leave him?

TITINIUS   All disconsolate,
With Pindarus his bondsman, on this hill.   60

Oh, coward am I to live so long
To see my best friend taken before my eyes.

Enter PINDARUS

Come here, fellow.
I took you prisoner in Parthia,
Saving your life, and made you swear,   40
That whatever I asked you to do,
You would do it. Come now, keep your oath.
You will be a free man, and with this good sword
That ran through Caesar's bowels, stab me in the heart.
Don't stop to argue. Here, take the hilt   45
And when my face is covered, as it is now,
Thrust the sword. [PINDARUS *stabs him*]
Caesar, you are revenged,
And with the very sword that killed you. [*Dies*]

PINDARUS So, I am free, yet would not have been   50
Had I dared to do as I wished. Oh, Cassius,
I shall run away from this country,
Where no Roman will ever find me.

Exits

Enter TITINIUS *and* MESSALA

MESSALA It is an even exchange, Titinius, for Octavius
Is defeated by the power of noble Brutus,   55
As the legions of Cassius are by Antony.

TITINIUS This news will greatly encourage Cassius.

MESSALA Where did you leave him?

TITINIUS Very dejected,
With his slave Pindarus, on this hill.   60

MESSALA Is not he that lies upon the ground?

TITINIUS He lies not like the living. O my heart!

MESSALA Is not that he?

TITINIUS No, this was he, Messala,

But Cassius is no more. O setting sun,　　　　　　　　　65

As in thy red rays thou dost sink to night,

So in his red blood Cassius' day is set.

The sun of Rome is set. Our day is gone,

Clouds, dews, and dangers come. Our deeds are done.

Mistrust of my success hath done this deed.　　　　　70

MESSALA Mistrust of good success hath done this deed.

O hateful error, melancholy's child,

Why dost thou show to the apt thoughts of men

The things that are not? O error, soon conceived,

Thou never com'st unto a happy birth　　　　　　　75

But kill'st the mother that engendered thee.

TITINIUS What, Pindarus? Where art thou, Pindarus?

MESSALA Seek him, Titinius, whilst I go to meet

The noble Brutus, thrusting this report

Into his ears. I may say "thrusting" it,　　　　　　80

For piercing steel and darts envenomed

Shall be as welcome to the ears of Brutus

As tidings of this sight.

TITINIUS Hie you, Messala,

And I will seek for Pindarus the while.　　　　　　85

[*Exit* MESSALA]

Why didst thou send me forth, brave Cassius?

Did I not meet thy friends? And did not they

MESSALA Isn't that he, lying on the ground?

TITINIUS He doesn't look alive. Oh, my heart!

MESSALA Isn't that he?

TITINIUS No, this was he, Messala.

>Cassius is no more. Oh, setting sun,   65
>
>Just as your rays turn red at nightfall,
>
>So in his red blood has Cassius' day ended.
>
>The sun of Rome is set. Our day is over—
>
>Clouds, vapors, and dangers come. Our role is ended.
>
>Doubt of my success has caused this.   70

MESSALA Doubt of great success has caused this.

>Oh, hateful error, the child of depression,
>
>Why do you show impressionable men
>
>Things that are not true? Oh, error, easily conceived,
>
>You never produce a happy birth,   75
>
>But kill the mother that bore you.

TITINIUS Where's Pindarus? Where are you, Pindarus?

MESSALA Look for him, Titinius, while I go to meet

>The noble Brutus and thrust the report of this
>
>Into his ears. I say "thrust"   80
>
>For sharp steel and poisoned lances
>
>Would be as welcome to the ears of Brutus
>
>As the news of this sight.

TITINIUS Hurry, Messala,

>And I will look for Pindarus.   85

>>   [*Exit* MESSALA]

>Why did you send me out, brave Cassius?
>
>Did I not meet with your friends? And did they not

Put on my brows this wreath of victory

And bid me give it thee? Didst thou not hear their shouts?

Alas, thou hast misconstrued everything. 90

But hold thee, take this garland on thy brow;

Thy Brutus bid me give it thee, and I

Will do his bidding. Brutus, come apace,

And see how I regarded Caius Cassius.

By your leave, gods, this is a Roman's part. 95

Come, Cassius' sword, and find Titinius' heart!

[*He kills himself*]

Alarum. Enter BRUTUS, MESSALA, YOUNG CATO,

VOLUMNIUS, LUCILIUS, LABEO, *and* FLAVIUS

BRUTUS Where, where, Messala, doth his body lie?

MESSALA Lo yonder, and Titinius mourning it.

BRUTUS Titinius' face is upward.

CATO He is slain. 100

BRUTUS O Julius Caesar, thou are mighty yet,

Thy spirit walks abroad and turns our swords

Into our own proper entrails.

Low Alarums.

CATO Brave Titinius!

Look whe'er he have not crowned dead Cassius. 105

BRUTUS Are yet two Romans living such as these?

The last of all the Romans, fare thee well!

It is impossible that ever Rome

Should breed thy fellow. Friends, I owe more tears

To this dead man than you shall see me pay. 110

I shall find time, Cassius, I shall find time.

Put on my head this wreath of victory
And ask that I give it to you? Didn't you hear their shouts?
Alas, you have misinterpreted everything. 90
But wait. Put this garland on your brow.
Your Brutus asked me to give it to you, and I
Will do as he asked. Brutus, come quickly,
And see how I honor Caius Cassius.
By your leave, gods, being a Roman requires it. 95
Come, Cassius' sword, and find Titinius' heart!

[*He kills himself*]

Sounds of battle. Enter BRUTUS, MESSALA, YOUNG CATO,
      VOLUMNIUS, LUCILIUS, LABEO, *and* FLAVIUS

BRUTUS   Where, where, Messala, does his body lie?

MESSALA   There, ahead, and Titinius is mourning it.

BRUTUS   Titinius is facing upward.

CATO   He is dead. 100

BRUTUS   Oh, Julius Caesar, you are mighty still,
    Your spirit walks the earth and turns our swords
    Into our very own bowels.

Low battle sounds.

CATO   Brave Titinius!
    Look, if he hasn't crowned dead Cassius. 105

BRUTUS   Are there still two Romans alive like these?
    The last of all the Romans, farewell!
    Rome shall never again
    Produce your equal. Friends, I owe more tears
    To this dead man than you will see me pay. 110
    I shall find time, Cassius, I shall find time.

Come therefore and to Thasos send his body;

His funerals shall not be in our camp

Lest it discomfort us. Lucilius, come,

And come, young Cato, let us to the field,   115

Labeo and Flavius, set our battles on.

'Tis three o'clock, and, Romans, yet ere night

We shall try fortune in a second fight.

Exeunt

Scene 4 [*The battlefield at Philippi*]

Alarum. Enter BRUTUS, MESSALA, YOUNG CATO,

      LUCILIUS, FLAVIUS, *and* LABEO

BRUTUS Yet, countrymen, O, yet hold up your heads!

[*Exits with* MESSALA, FLAVIUS, *and* LABEO, *fighting*]

CATO What bastard doth not? Who will go with me?

I will proclaim my name about the field.

I am the son of Marcus Cato, ho!

A foe to tyrants, and my country's friend.   5

I am the son of Marcus Cato, ho!

Enter SOLDIERS *and fight*

LUCILIUS And I am Brutus, Marcus Brutus, I,

Brutus, my country's friend. Know me for Brutus!

[YOUNG CATO *is killed*]

O young and noble Cato, art thou down?

Why, now thou diest as bravely as Titinius   10

And mayst be honored, being Cato's son.

FIRST SOLDIER Yield, or thou diest.

LUCILIUS Only I yield to die.

Therefore, let us go; and send his body to Thasos.

His funeral shall not take place in our camp,

Lest it dishearten our army. Lucilius, come,

And come, young Cato, let us go to the battlefield.   115

Labeo and Flavius, order our forces to advance.

It's three o'clock, and Romans, before this night,

We shall try our luck in a second fight.

Exit all

Scene 4 [*The battlefield at Philippi*]

Battle sounds. Enter BRUTUS, MESSALA, YOUNG CATO,

        LUCILIUS, FLAVIUS, *and* LABEO

BRUTUS Still, countrymen, Oh, still hold up your heads.

        [*Exits with* MESSALA, FLAVIUS, *and* LABEO, *fighting*]

CATO Who is so low born, he will not? Who will go with me?

    I will shout my name about the field.

    I am the son of Marcus Cato, yes!

    An enemy of tyrants, and my country's friend.   5

    I am the son of Marcus Cato, yes!

            Enter SOLDIERS *and fight*

LUCILIUS And I am Brutus, Marcus Brutus I am,

    Brutus, my country's friend. I am Brutus, as you see!

    [YOUNG CATO *is killed*]

    Oh, young and noble Cato, have you fallen?

    Why, you died as bravely as Titinius   10

    And, as you are Cato's son, honor is yours.

FIRST SOLDIER Yield, or you die.

LUCILIUS I yield only to die.

There is so much that thou wilt kill me straight.

Kill Brutus and be honored in his death. 15

FIRST SOLDIER We must not. A noble prisoner!

Enter ANTONY

SECOND SOLDIER Room ho! Tell Antony, Brutus is ta'en.

FIRST SOLDIER I'll tell the news. Here comes the general.

Brutus is ta'en, Brutus is ta'en, my lord!

ANTONY Where is he? 20

LUCILIUS Safe, Antony, Brutus is safe enough.

I dare assure thee that no enemy

Shall ever take alive the noble Brutus.

The gods defend him from so great a shame!

When you do find him, or alive or dead, 25

He will be found like Brutus, like himself.

ANTONY This is not Brutus, friend, but I assure you,

A prize no less in worth. Keep this man safe,

Give him all kindness. I had rather have

Such men my friends than enemies. Go on, 30

And see where Brutus be alive or dead,

And bring us word unto Octavius' tent

How everything is chanced.

Exeunt

Scene 5 [*Another part of the battlefield*]

Enter BRUTUS, DARDANIUS, CLITUS, STRATO, *and* VOLUMNIUS

BRUTUS Come, poor remains of friends, rest on this rock.

CLITUS Statilius showed the torchlight but, my lord,

He came not back. He is or ta'en or slain.

There is ample reason for you to kill me at once.

You kill Brutus and will be honored for his death.   15

FIRST SOLDIER We must not. Not a noble prisoner!

Enter ANTONY

SECOND SOLDIER Make way! Tell Antony, Brutus is taken.

FIRST SOLDIER I'll tell him. Here comes the general.

Brutus is taken, Brutus is taken, my lord!

ANTONY Where is he?   20

LUCILIUS Safe, Antony. Brutus is safe enough.

I can assure you that no enemy

Shall ever take the noble Brutus alive.

The gods defend him from so great a shame!

When you do find him, either alive or dead,   25

He will be found like Brutus, true to himself.

ANTONY This is not Brutus, friend, but I assure you,

He is a prize as valuable. Keep this man safe,

Give him all kindness. I had rather have

Such men my friends than my enemies. Go now,   30

And see whether Brutus is alive or dead.

And bring word to us in Octavius' tent

How everything turned out.

They exit

Scene 5 [*Another part of the battlefield*]

Enter BRUTUS, DARDANIUS, CLITUS, STRATO, *and* VOLUMNIUS

BRUTUS Come, wretched survivors, rest on this rock.

CLITUS Statilius waved the signal light but, my lord,

He has not come back. He is either taken or killed,

BRUTUS Sit thee down, Clitus. Slaying is the word,

It is a deed in fashion. Hark thee, Clitus. [*Whispers*]   5

CLITUS What, I, my lord? No, not for all the world.

BRUTUS Peace then, no words.

CLITUS I'll rather kill myself.

BRUTUS Hark thee, Dardanius. [*Whispers*]

DARDANIUS Shall I do such a deed?   10

CLITUS O Dardanius!

DARDANIUS O Clitus!

CLITUS What ill request did Brutus make to thee?

DARDANIUS To kill him, Clitus. Look, he meditates.

CLITUS Now is that noble vessel full of grief,   15

That it runs over even at his eyes.

BRUTUS Come hither, good Volumnius, list a word.

VOLUMNIUS What says my lord?

BRUTUS Why, this, Volumnius.

The ghost of Caesar hath appeared to me   20

Two several times by night, at Sardis once

And this last night here in Philippi fields.

I know my hour is come.

VOLUMNIUS Not so, my lord.

BRUTUS Nay, I am sure it is, Volumnius.   25

Thou seest the world, Volumnius, how it goes.

Our enemies have beat us to the pit.

Low Alarums.

It is more worthy to leap in ourselves

Than tarry till they push us. Good Volumnius,

Thou know'st that we two went to school together.   30

BRUTUS   Sit down here, Clitus. Killing is the right word.

It is a fashionable thing to do. Listen, Clitus. [*Whispers*]   5

CLITUS   What, me, my lord? No, not for all the world.

BRUTUS   Quiet, then. Say nothing about this.

CLITUS   I'd rather kill myself.

BRUTUS   A word with you, Dardanius. [*Whispers*]

DARDANIUS   Should I do such a thing?   10

CLITUS   Oh, Dardanius!

DARDANIUS   Oh, Clitus!

CLITUS   What hard thing did Brutus ask you to do?

DARDANIUS   To kill him, Clitus. Look how he broods.

CLITUS   That noble vessel is so full of grief   15

That it overflows his eyes.

BRUTUS   Come here, good Volumnius, and listen to me.

VOLUMNIUS   My lord, what do you have to say?

BRUTUS   Why, this, Volumnius.

The ghost of Caesar has appeared to me   20

Twice at night, once at Sardis

And last night, here on the Philippi field.

I know my hour has come.

VOLUMNIUS   That's not so, my lord.

BRUTUS   No, Volumnius, I am sure it is.   25

You see the world, Volumnius, and how things turn out.

Our enemies have driven us to the edge.

Low battle sounds.

It is more honorable to leap into the grave ourselves

Than wait until they push us. Good Volumnius,

You remember we went to school together.   30

Even for that our love of old, I prithee

Hold thou my sword-hilts whilst I run on it.

VOLUMNIUS   That's not an office for a friend, my lord.

Alarum still.

CLITUS   Fly, fly, my lord, there is no tarrying here.

BRUTUS   Farewell to you, and you, and you, Volumnius.   35

Strato, thou hast been all this while asleep.

Farewell to thee too, Strato. Countrymen,

My heart doth joy that yet in all my life

I found no man but he was true to me.

I shall have glory by this losing day   40

More than Octavius and Mark Antony

By this vile conquest shall attain unto.

So fare you well at once, for Brutus' tongue

Hath almost ended his life's history.

Night hangs upon mine eyes, my bones would rest,   45

That have but labored to attain this hour.

Alarum. Cry within, "Fly, fly, fly!"

CLITUS   Fly, my lord, fly!

BRUTUS   Hence! I will follow.

>   [*Exit* CLITUS, DARDANIUS, *and* VOLUMNIUS]

I prithee, Strato, stay thou by thy lord.

Thou are a fellow of a good respect,   50

Thy life hath had some smatch of honor in it.

Hold then my sword and turn away thy face,

While I do run upon it. Wilt thou, Strato?

STRATO   Give me your hand first. Fare you well, my lord.

Just for the sake of our old friendship, I beg you

Hold the hilt of my sword while I run on it.

VOLUMNIUS That's not a task for a friend, my lord.

Sounds of battle grow loud.

CLITUS Run, run, my lord, there is no staying here.

BRUTUS Farewell to you, and you, and you, Volumnius.   35

Strato, you have been asleep the whole time.

Farewell to you too, Strato. Countrymen,

My heart rejoices that in all my life

I have known no man who was untrue to me.

I shall have on this day of defeat more glory   40

Than either Octavius or Mark Antony

By their evil conquest can claim.

So farewell all of you, for Brutus' tongue

Has nearly ended his story.

Night hangs upon my eyes, my bones that have   45

Labored to bring me to this final hour, seek rest.

Sounds of battle. Cry within, "Run. run, run!"

CLITUS Run, my lord, run!

BRUTUS Go on, I will follow.

[*Exit* CLITUS, DARDANIUS, *and* VOLUMNIUS]

I ask you, Strato, to stay with your lord.

You are a man of good reputation,   50

Your life has had some touch of honor in it.

Turn your face away and hold my sword

While I run on it. Will you do this, Strato?

STRATO Give me your hand first. Farewell, my lord.

BRUTUS   Farewell, good Strato.   55

[*Runs on his sword*]

Caesar, now be still,

I killed not thee with half so good a will. [*Dies*]

Alarum. Retreat. Enter ANTONY, OCTAVIUS,

      MESSALA, LUCILIUS, *and the* ARMY

OCTAVIUS   What man is that?

MESSALA   My master's man. Strato, where is thy master?

STRATO   Free from the bondage you are in, Messala.   60

The conquerors can but make a fire of him,

For Brutus only overcame himself,

And no man else hath honor by his death.

LUCILIUS   So Brutus should be found. I thank thee, Brutus,

That thou hast proved Lucilius' saying true.   65

OCTAVIUS   All that served Brutus, I will entertain them.

Fellow, wilt thou bestow thy time with me?

STRATO   Ay, if Messala will prefer me to you.

OCTAVIUS   Do so, good Messala.

MESSALA   How died my master, Strato?   70

STRATO   I held the sword, and he did run on it.

MESSALA   Octavius, then take him to follow thee,

That did the latest service to my master.

ANTONY   This was the noblest Roman of them all.

All the conspirators, save only he,   75

Did that they did in envy of great Caesar.

He only, in the general honest thought

And common good to all, made one of them.

BRUTUS   Farewell, good Strato.   55

[*Runs on his sword*]

Caesar, now be at peace,

I killed you not half so willingly. [*Dies*]

Battle sounds. Trumpet signals an end. Enter ANTONY,
        OCTAVIUS, MESSALA, LUCILIUS, *and the* ARMY

OCTAVIUS   Who is that man?

MESSALA   My master's servant. Strato, where is your master?

STRATO   Free from the bondage you are in, Messala.   60

The conquerors can only make a bonfire of him,

For Brutus has defeated himself,

And no man can claim the victory of his death.

LUCILIUS   That's how Brutus should be found. Thank you, Brutus,

For proving me right when I said you'd never be taken alive.   65

OCTAVIUS   Those who served Brutus, I will ask to serve me.

Fellow, are you willing to give me your time?

STRATO   Yes, if Messala will recommend me to you.

OCTAVIUS   Do so, good Messala.

MESSALA   How did my master die, Strato?   70

STRATO   I held the sword, and he ran on it.

MESSALA   Octavius, then take him to serve you.

He did my master the final service.

ANTONY   This was the noblest Roman of them all.

All of the conspirators, except him,   75

Did what they did out of envy of great Caesar.

He, only in an honest belief that he was serving

The common good, became one of them.

His life was gentle, and the elements
So mixed in him that Nature might stand up   80
And say to the world, "This was a man."
OCTAVIUS According to his virtue, let us use him,
    With all respect, and rites of burial.
    Within my tent his bones tonight shall lie,
    Most like a soldier, ordered honorably.   85
    So call the field to rest, and let's away
    To part the glories of this happy day.

Exeunt

His life was noble. His qualities
So well balanced that Nature might stand up   80
And say to all the world, "This was a man."
OCTAVIUS Let us treat him with the honor he deserves,
With all due respect and rites of burial.
Within my tent his body shall lie tonight,
Like a true soldier, treated with honor.   85
Order the fighting to stop, let's go away
To share the glories of this happy day.

They all exit

Glossary

The following terms are taken from the translation of *The Tragedy of Julius Caesar*. The scene and line numbers are given in parentheses after the terms, which are listed in the order they first occur.

Act One

Pompey (scene 1, line 38): popular Roman general, allied with Caesar in the First Triumvirate (ruling group of three), who sided with the Senate against Caesar and fled Rome when Caesar returned and became dictator. Pompey was murdered in Egypt

River Tiber (scene 1, line 46): begins in central Italy and flows through Rome to its mouth at Ostia

Pompey's sons (scene 1, line 52): Gnaeus and Sextus, leaders of the last pocket of armed resistance to Caesar, defeated at the battle of Munda; the play opens with Caesar's triumphant return to Rome

Feast of Lupercal (scene 1, line 68): originally, a festival in honor of Lupercus (the god Pan), protector of flocks and herds; later, the festival adopted by Rome to ward off evil spirits

Lupercal race (scene 2, line 6): Young men dressed only in goat skins ran a course through the city of Rome on the Feast of Lupercal, and barren women touched by them were believed to become fertile

ides of March (scene 2, line 21): March 15

Aeneas (scene 2, line 118): legendary hero who carried his father Anchises from the burning city of Troy and subsequently sailed to Italy and founded Rome

Titinius (scene 2, line 133): a friend and an ally of Cassius and Brutus

colossus (scene 2, line 142): giant bronze statue of the sun god Apollo whose legs, according to legend, spanned the harbor at Rhodes; one of the seven wonders of the world

great flood (scene 2, line 158): both the Bible and classical literature relate the story of a universal flood, in which only one virtuous couple was spared to renew the human race

Brutus (scene 2, line 165): Lucius Junius Brutus who, in legend, drove out the ancient kings of Rome and helped found the Republic of Rome, and from whom Brutus claimed descent

Cicero (scene 2, line 192): leading orator and statesman of Rome

falling-sickness (scene 2, line 258): epilepsy, a disorder of the central nervous system, often marked by convulsive attacks

bird of night (scene 3, line 26): owl

Pompey's theatre (scene 3, line 130): first public theatre built by Pompey, located outside the gates of Rome

alchemy (scene 3, line 164): medieval science concerned with turning lesser metals into gold

Act Two

Tarquin (scene 1, line 54): king of Rome, expelled from power by an ancestor of Brutus

Erebus (scene 1, line 87): region between earth and Hades, the underworld of classical mythology

unicorns (scene 1, line 214): according to legend, hunters tricked this mythical animal by dodging away from a tree so that the unicorn ran its horn into the trunk, entrapping itself

Cato (scene 1, line 306): an orator and a statesman, he fought for Pompey in the civil war and committed suicide to avoid capture by Caesar; he was Portia's father

praetors (scene 4, line 39): Roman judges

Act Three

Olympus (scene 1, line 80): mountain range in Greece; in mythology, the home of the gods

Ate (scene 1, line 290): Greek goddess of discord and destruction

Cry Havoc (scene 1, line 291): the order to kill without mercy, an order that only a king could give

dogs of war (scene 1, line 291): identified in Shakespeare's *Henry V* as famine, sword, and fire

Nervii (scene 2, line 176): a tribe in Gaul, which Caesar defeated in 57 B.C., one of his greatest victories

drachmas (scene 2, line 247): silver coins; seventy-five drachmas was a large sum

Act Four

Pluto's mine (scene 3, line 111): Pluto was the god of the underworld and also of gold and silver mines, and of corn

Philippi (scene 3, line 190): a town in Macedonia

Act Five

red flag (scene 1, line 15): the Roman signal for battle

Hybla (scene 1, line 36): a town in Sicily famous for its honey

Epicurus (scene 1, line 84): Greek philosopher who advocated simple living and denied the influence of the supernatural

Parthia (scene 3, line 39): scene of battle, now in modern Iran

Thasos (scene 3, line 112): an island in Greece near Philippi